The Knopf Poetry Series

Also by Pamela White Hadas

The Passion of Lilith

Marianne Moore (A Study)

Designing Women

In Light of Genesis

BESIDE HERSELF

BESIDE HERSELF
Pocahontas
to Patty Hearst

POEMS BY

Pamela White Hadas

Alfred A. Knopf   New York   1983

THIS IS A BORZOI BOOK
PUBLISHED BY ALFRED A. KNOPF, INC.

I wish to express my deepest heartfelt thanks to Stanley Elkin, in whose carrel in
Olin Library most of this book was written. My gratitude is due also to The
MacDowell Colony and the Corporation of Yaddo for allowing me special space
and time in which to work. To my colleagues at the Bread Loaf Writers'
Conference, and to the audiences there, I also owe a great debt.

Some of the poems in this collection originally appeared in the following
magazines: *American Poetry Review, The Kenyon Review, New England
Review/Breadloaf Quarterly, Poet & Critic, River Styx, Tendril, TriQuarterly,*
and *West Branch*. "To Make a Dragon Move: From the Diary of an Anorexic,"
"Ringling Bros. Present: The Lucky Lucie Lamort," and excerpts from "The
Bandit Queen Remembers" originally appeared in *Poetry*.

Library of Congress Cataloging in Publication Data

Hadas, Pamela White.   Beside herself.

    (Knopf poetry series ; 12)
    1. Women—United States—Poetry.   I. Title.
PS3558.A311598B4   1983   811'.54   82-49003
ISBN 0-394-52993-6   ISBN 0-394-71343-5 (pbk.)

Manufactured in the United States of America

FIRST EDITION

For Alice, China, Joan, Judy and Naomi

and for all who have known themselves beside themselves

and for David, who is beside me most

We feel after our fate in the lines of other lives, and for this learning it matters little whether those figures be real, as we say, or imagined, so that they live.

—*Elizabeth Sewell, "Cosmos and Kingdom"*

CONTENTS

∿

The use of this symbol indicates a
stanza break at the bottom of the page.

ix

BESIDE HERSELF

POCAHONTAS FROM HER NEW WORLD

1   To Powhatan

Dear, great Powhatan, father, I would write
news to you of this new world, and yet,
the deepest syllables that I might use
are nowhere written. There's no alphabet
between us, only the sound low as the tide
in a shell's ear—your voice calming me to sleep
with explanations of the world that came
to me as my own dreams, my secret name . . .
　　　(My husband John surprises me. "What's this?"
　　　he asks me, "Is the Princess Pocahontas
　　　not satisfied, the royal belle of London,
　　　but she must scribble, too, and prove the savage
　　　can compete with Shakespeare?" I insist
　　　I am but writing for my father. "Ha!"
　　　quoth my husband, "Do you think Powhatan
　　　is learning so much English in your absence?"
　　　"His tongue has not the script nor words I need,"
　　　say I, "It is a letter for myself.
　　　I feign it is for him so I may say
　　　what else I might not say of what I see."
　　　"You've learned to talk in riddles," says John then,
　　　"Nothing proves the influence more strongly
　　　of courts and courtly foolishness. I fear
　　　you may have learned the use of words too well.
　　　Yet, go on." He chucks my chin. "But for you
　　　King James would not approve our sweet tobacco.")

　　　(I carry a small light globe inside of me
　　　at the center of my body and as I move
　　　it steadies my senses, still, among snailshells

and silkgrass, back straight and belly flat,
stringing cranberries on nettle fiber,
scooping light into dolls of clay or wood . . .)

The Earl of Buckingham is next to me
in the royal box. The Globe is full.
The rumors of our romance are all lies.
Is there nowhere where I will not be
surrounded, where I can unfold myself
the daughter of the moon and tidewater
in ancient syllables to the ancient soul
that is my personal treasure, still? O, God,
gather up my smiles and courtesies
and all the toys and trials and toils of being
an explorer. Tell me how to tell
Powhatan what I am beholding here,
in this new world, this Globe, this startling stage.
There's Jessica and Juliet together,
somehow sharing the center of my dream
of infinite translations . . . Do I love
a loathèd enemy? . . .

    (I hide that little mirror, that Captain Smith
     gave me, through you, long ago. I make
     my eyes into his eyes seeing me. How we fall
     in love is mystery and has to do
     with mirrors, I think; with mirrors I move
     outside myself . . .)

I must work to understand some jokes.
Prince Charles explains: the maidens, fish and weapons,
bitten thumbs, the have-at-thees and down-
with-those, the flourishes and purple fountains . . .
They touch here palm to palm and lip to cheek.
In sooth, I know not why I am so sad . . .
The Earl of Somerset's lips against my hand

shock me no more, nor the painted blue
veins on wide bare bosoms. Diamonds burn
in and out from my burnished skin. I cannot
move but hands reach out to touch my cape . . .
Their painted eyes forever hunting me . . .
Did I deny my father and refuse my name?

    (I see Powhatan standing on the shore
      as, flag-strung and square-rigged we float away
      from the spume-flecked dunes. We each grow small in each
      other's eyes. His sadness is moon-faced . . .)

Here's trifling foolish banquets, torchlight, lutes,
fantastics, antics, counterfeits, prick songs . . .
The Earl of Pembroke quaffs the fume and chats
throughout the play—he's all embroidery,
pompoms and glitter, gold-clocked hose . . . I see
comedy and tragedy together:
Tomocomo in his beads and feathers
plays his part, clay-daubed, proud of his crown
of snake and weasel skins . . . while I dress up
in shoes that pinch and petticoats and crushed
velvet. Who's best on stage? These daughters leave
their fathers, all for love . . .

    (I have not forgotten how to stitch with bone,
      make porcupine and oyster stew. I long
      for my bed of pine boughs in Virginia, long
      for the clean river at dawn, my skin
      open to Ahone: I long for my clearing,
      the trees mothering at the edge, the moon washing down,
      my father's voice . . .)

I cannot hear you say my baptised name:
Rebecca, Lady Rebecca Rolfe . . . I ask
one of King James' translators what it means,

Rebecca: it means to bind, means beautiful—
as animals noosed for sacrifice: that is,
binding as a promise, perhaps, of plenty
should God fulfill . . . binding as blood, my own
mixed with my husband's in Thomas' veins.
You see, I do not like a strict translation.
Pocahontas means more than your playful wanton.
It means to risk, means to explore the world,
to dress as for a play and play it out
so far as beasts bound in crinolines and lace
can play, and this brings peace, as my baptism
did, to Jamestown and your warriors,
if not to me. I dream of no return.

I rave, the London air has poisoned me,
but not before I see the gaiety
and gore, the silly splendid rituals . . .
You argue in me, rage, and yet you want
the fortune of new things. The sea between us
is the vast between myself and myself.
You let me go . . . You stood there on the shore . . .
I am a native of the world, confused.
How does one piece the old and new together
but by separations, explorations
down to the seed that's shared (I rave, I know . . .)
in the crossing of two strains, the grief and joy
that makes one wild to see the ends of things
and the beginnings that are the ends of words
between us, father, to let the renegade bloom,
reborn into the earth's womb once more where
I am Pocahontas, wanton; Rebecca, bound;
and something else, not old or new, but found.

II   *To Captain John Smith*

Dear Captain Smith, they told me you were dead,
and I believed, despite my deeper sense
that we would meet again, and here you are
in London. Badly dressed and bungling
your apologies for leaving me
with no farewell . . .

     (John Rolfe is looking over my shoulder again.
     "Another letter? When you should rest yourself!
     Aren't the deaths of half your retinue
     of 'Naturals' enough to frighten you?"
     He puts his careful hand against my cheek.
     "You're burning up! Or is this blush because
     your letter, as I note, is for John Smith,
     that antagonistic foolish man.
     His creditors will get him yet, you know.
     When he called here you hid your face,
     had not a word to say, so what is this?"
     "It is a letter for myself," quoth I,
     "it's not for him or you or anyone . . .
     Sometimes writing something makes it clear,
     and there's so much that is unclear to me."
     "Go on, but if I hear you cough once more,
     I'll take your quill and ink away for good."
     He goes and I try to find the thread again
     of what I need must say . . .)

Some called you hero, some impostor, I
care not how many battles won or lost,

how many Turkish maidens you've seduced,
whose blood is on your hands for good or ill.
You are like all men in claiming such,
and I write to you as I would write to all
men of the world, you who take yourselves
so seriously, you who cannot talk
but you end up arguing. I overheard
the squabbles, rumpus, brawls in Fort Jamestown.
I overheard my brothers' ruckus, too.
You could not agree among yourselves just how
to hate the strangeness of another world
suddenly exposed. I have to laugh
when I recall the horror on your face,
you who brag of being a soldier to the Prince
of Transylvania, so worldly-wise,
when you came upon our harvest dance,
the maidens naked but for horns and paint
dancing the ring of fire, and led by me.
Oh, yes, I had my eye on you that night.
You were the magic man whose little mirror
my father gave to me, whose knives are sharp.
We sit and suck sweet cobs together, you
teach me new words: for food, for dance, for moon.
My father and my brothers glare at you.
We do not touch. Your eyes are shifty, bright.
I smell your skin, your fear. I want to tease
you as I tease my brothers. I want to show
you how cleanly I use a bow and arrow,
how swiftly swim and climb the Jamestown steeple . . .

> (A man, a bear, a dragon, and a leopard
> protect Powhatan's temple, copper, corn . . .
> My father has such hidden trackless power . . .

We are the tallest tribe, the tidewater
belongs to us. What can a stranger do
but give new toys and powers to Powhatan's daughter?)

That was my innocence. Not long before
I had been waiting for my womanhood
away from men, in the longhouse of the maidens.
Free, I find my way to Wingandacoa
through moonflowers, flaming foxglove, whortleberries.
I dress as a boy in Werowocomoco,
attend my father's Council. Secretly,
I kill my first wild pig, I skin a snake.
Men talk of doing this to other men.
I am the eyes between the leaves. I listen
for more than rabbit, porcupine and fox.
I listen for strange words: *to starve, to die.*
I see splendors and atrocities
in two worlds and I am torn between . . .
I see your secret burials. I pity you,
God's handful, eating your bitter bread, but most
I want my wizard Smith to hold his own,
the man of mirrors, of thunders, man of words.
You show me cloth, shoes, knives and forks and beds.
So I bring food and I bring warnings, too,
through snow and bramble, against Powhatan's will.

(My body shakes with laughter as I stand
for the first time before the Lady de la Warre's
pierglass, draped in her silk dress, until
Tomakin sees, glares blackly from the mirror
to me and rips the yellow silk from my body,
still shaking. My Lady screams, and I see how
serious a masquerade can be . . .)

Soon after, your bulwarks crumble, palisades
split wide. I see your rabble, huddled, panged
and perishing; I see Powhatan's glee.
And then you're gone, wounded, so they say,
and in disgrace. They tell me you are dead,
and they whisper other things when they see my grief—
how you might have married me, in short.
It was not for that, my grief; my grief
was that you were no more than other men.
I saw that even Powhatan . . . I was young . . .
But it is foolish to discuss such lies,
now I am John Rolfe's wife and Thomas' mother.
And still, and still, I have to know one thing.
It's whispered here in London, you have told
how Powhatan meant to sacrifice
your life, and when your head was on the stone,
Pocahontas flung herself upon you,
took your head in her arms and saved your life.
Did you dream it?

    (I recall the dream. It made me blush,
      forbidden as I was to touch a man,
      much less a *tassentasse*. And yet your hair,
      so coarse and wild with firelight, face
      so hot, the sense of your whole trembling form
      stretched out—the power, vulnerability—
      stayed with me many days. I told no one.
      I was ashamed, and rapt.)

That's why I hid my face the other day,
partly—it was not only shame, but just
confusion, one dream coming to us both,
a dream that isolates . . . no, compromises . . .

no, I don't know what . . . you are so changed.
And I am changed. I am a Lady now.
I've been to Whitehall, Hampton Court, masked balls.
And you are something faded, out of touch.
I don't want our dream, and yet I do.
But why make the story simpler than it was,
lose that touch-and-go between us, all
the bafflement? Something in me always
wanted to pull back, forget the dream.
And even now, I want to hide. I want
to hate what pulls me out of myself, away
from the wildwood's quiet, beginning with that dream
that is not mine alone, that makes me seem
sometimes hero, sometimes impostor, just like you.
You funny man, you fallen thing, what a tangle
of worlds you have brought me to, and what an end . . .
of masquerade, toys, powers, enmities
and surprising peace, dear impostor, dear friend.

III   *To John Rolfe*

Dear Husband, when you thought to marry me
despite your aweful trembling at the thought
of God's displeasure with the sons of Levi
for marrying strange wives, you wrote a letter
to Sir Thomas Dale, our friend. He showed
that letter to me. I never mentioned it
for fear you would shy away from me . . .

> (Can I not sit down with quill and ink
>   but John must come and read my stiff beginning?

"You saw my letter? Why confess it now?"
"For fear that you would shy away from me
at the thought your soul had been exposed to one
whom you still thought beneath your love," say I.
"It wasn't that, Rebecca, I was afraid,
and that was three years ago, or more, and now
God's will is plain to me, the Colony
at peace with Powhatan, tobacco flourishing . . .
What have you got to say to me that you
must write it out, and in your weak condition?"
"I must write because I'm going to die.
I must fashion coherent memory,
these years have gone so fast." I bite
my tongue to keep from crying out to him
to save me, but there's nothing he can do.
"I've had a dream," I say, "my father was
on the Pamunkey shore scattering beads
among my people. I lay wrapped in doeskin
with food and water for the journey, pearls
and my little mirror. I saw my brothers blacken
their faces and howl . . ." "Tell me no dreams," says John,
"of savage things. You are in London now,
a Lady, blessed, beloved of God and me.
Remember this, if you must write." He turns
and goes. I hear the sob caught in his throat.)

What a lot we had to teach each other.
All your meditations and your prayers
were matched by mine. It was no easier
for me to reconcile my rebellious love.
Remember how I came to Henrico, bound
as hostage, dressed in unfamiliar clothes,
preached to in a language I not yet
fully understood. I asked myself,
was I stolen or did I give myself?

I went to feast on Captain Argall's ship
of my own free will. I was still curious
about the growing Colony, although
I had some news from Father's hostages.
They were to be my ransom, with stolen arms
and corn, should Powhatan have valued me
at that price. I try to remember now
how I was torn . . .

    (All the sacred places, faces, gods,
       the grapevines swung upon, the cartwheels turned,
       the running wild, the daily swim, the calm . . .
       And then the pale men in their finery,
       the ringing bells, the Reverend Whitaker's
       softly instructing voice, the land beyond,
       with all its mysteries . . .)

And then I met you at the Jamestown Church.
I carried my Horn Book with its alphabet
and Lord's Prayer. You asked the Reverend
if you might help me with the Catechism.
Why was I created? You had to ask yourself
as much as I. Was it to love, or work
in God's vineyard? Had Satan struck your heart
with his hot hoof? Your passions, sufferings,
were matched by mine. I knew I lay between
your God and your secret heart, your dusky love,
your persimmon, your godly tax, your dream
that wakes you to astonishment, still,
as God takes you by the hand and you take mine.

    (I stand before the altar in my Dacca muslin,
       the same I wore to be baptised Rebecca,
       Powhatan's absence as a wound in me,
       Powhatan's gift of freshwater pearls around

my neck, a white ivory comb in my hair,
and with my body I thee worship, said
and done, the "Peace of Pocahontas," done.)

I was no longer "rude and barbarous,"
my "generation cursed," etcetera . . .
I told you when to tap the maple tree.
You showed me the tiny Trinidado seed.
I told you in which thickets the turkeys hid.
You taught me how to spin, make cheese and candles.
I showed you roots and leaves and barks that heal.
I knew migrations, spawnings; you knew books
and theatre. We planted corn and beans
in the same plot, together, crossed our strains . . .

(And soon I come to term and slip away
to the forest with my sisters, aunts,
to bear our child, to dip him in the river
as Powhatan's heir must be, to bind him,
wrapped in warm skins, to the cradleboard.)

You see how Thomas likes his wooden hoop
and hobbyhorse. He is as English as
he is Powhatan. Do you recall the verse
in Genesis: "And the Lord said unto her,
Two nations are in thy womb." The name
Rebecca is truly mine . . . I could go on
and on if I were stronger, my love . . .
I see how we were meant to be an emblem
beyond ourselves, beyond the weeping weather
of London, the present . . . It is enough the child
lives, to return my blood to Virginia's shore.
All my dreams are departures now, just as

my life . . . I feel as swift and deep and wide
as the Thames, I loop past Greenwich, Halfway Reach,
past the chalky cliffs of Gravesend where . . .
It's hard to breathe, and you must read my mind . . .

    (. . . hedgerows blossom, and lilacs. Prince Charles calls
    me sister, I understand his burdens well . . .
    hostages dismembered at the feast,
    the bite of meat spit out, the sacrifice . . .
    I am a work of grief and cambric . . . hold me.)

You say this is a julep of unicorn's horn,
powdered with pearl and a stag's heart's bone?
It's useless, my love, it is a fairy tale.

    (It is all for nothing and everything, I dream
    his golden bearded head in my arms . . . what worm
    is embedded in my body . . . smoke and feathers
    surround this hammock, a lace across the sea,
    a web to catch me with my ancient eyes . . .
    I am beyond and behind myself, sweet John,
    I hear the bells of St. George toll . . . I nod
    and curtsey, play hide-and-seek with the Queen
    where grass is clipped and counted trees are pruned . . .
    how many different kinds of maze . . . is this
    once more the Twelfth Night Masque where dreams have wings
    and dreams have honey and dreams have stings all come
    from a moving cloud and bower of flowers
    breaking open inside of me . . . I go . . .)

    go out upon the sea where nothing is
    written, but the thought becomes a wave
    in a lack-brain turbulence . . . where nothing is

spoken above the wind that blows beyond
myself and beyond myself I balance, ride
a sleep of sad motions and an edge
of piercing beauty, of kneeling in moonlight
where I am yet to be stolen, given away
where my father and my husband and my son
kneel beside the mother I must have had
her arms around and around and around me now

BETSY ROSS
IN THIRTEEN STATES OF MIND   *for Stephen Post*

By the needle you shall draw the thread, and by that which is past,
see how that which is to come will be drawn on.   —*Proverb*

It was in the latter part of May, 1776, that Washington, accompanied by
Colonel George Ross, a member of his staff, and by the Honorable
Robert Morris, the great financier of the revolution, called upon Mrs.
Betsy Ross, a niece of Colonel Ross. She was a young and beautiful
widow, only twenty-four years of age, and known to be expert at needle
work. They called to engage her services in preparing our first starry
flag. . . . It was here, in this house, that Washington unfolded a paper
on which had been rudely sketched a plan of a flag of thirteen stripes,
with a blue field dotted with thirteen stars. They talked over the plan of
this flag in detail, and Mrs. Ross noticed that the stars which were
sketched were six-pointed, and suggested that they should have five
points. Washington admitted that she was correct, but he preferred a
star that would not be an exact copy of that on his coat of arms, and he
also thought that a six-pointed star would be easier to cut. Mrs. Ross
liked the five-pointed star, and to show that they were easily cut she
deftly folded a piece of paper and with one clip of her scissors unfolded
a perfect star with five points . . .

From *The Story Of Our Flag, with Historical Sketch of the Quakeress
Betsy Ross,* by Addie Guthrie Weaver—a distant relative of Betsy Ross,
published by A. G. Weaver, Chicago, 1898, pp. 8–10.

The first public assertion that Betsy Ross made the first Stars and Stripes
appeared in a paper read before the Historical Society of Pennsylvania
on March 14, 1870, by William J. Canby, a grandson. However, Mr.
Canby on later investigation found no official documents of any action
by Congress on the flag before June 14, 1777. . . . The only actual record
of the manufacture of flags by Betsy Ross is a voucher in Harrisburg,
Pa., for 14 pounds and some shillings for flags for the Pennsylvania navy.

From the *Information Please Almanac, Atlas and Yearbook,* edited by
Ann Golenpaul, Simon and Schuster, New York, 1976, p. 518.

I

*—establishing with Powers so disposed—in order to give to trade
a stable course, . . . —conventional rules of intercourse; the best that
present circumstances and mutual opinion will permit, but
temporary, and liable to be from time to time abandoned or varied,
as experience and circumstances shall dictate; . . .*

Some say I made it up. Some say not so.
So what? I know that I relive the day—
late May—and may forever—when I met you
with Uncle Ross and Rich Rob. Secretly,

you'd brought me a little piecework to be done
for love and money. I put the kettle on
(for hardly any tea) and we sat down
hush hush—and you brought out the general plan

for a banner, this smudgy doodle you'd made—
not bad. At first I didn't like the a-
symmetry of it. "Too many seams," I said,
"and who wants six-point stars?" I showed how they
could be cut to five: one fold, one snip. I won.
You got your way about the stripes.
                                        Tomorrow, then.

Unless otherwise indicated, the epigraphs preceding the poems are quoted
from notes Washington sent to Hamilton pertaining to an address (which
became the Farewell Address), sent on May 15, 1792; and from the
Farewell Address itself, delivered in September, 1796.

II

*Taking care always to keep ourselves, by suitable establishments,
on a respectable defensive posture, we may safely trust to temporary
alliances for extraordinary emergencies.*

You came and went and left me with your plan.
        It was heavenly.
(Still, Mother Nature's waited on this man,
      & God knows so have I.)

All my tricks were ready for your trade:
        seed-stem-crewel-cross-chain
stitch—for you, for me, all signified . . .

        Cut and come again:

You came, to pick it up where you left off.
        You were down to earth
about the price: it's—give or take some—life,
        and all that one was worth . . .

And what a thing to fly
            with you—our seams
far spread-eagle fused—
          our scissions eclipsed.

III

Declare ye among the nations, and publish, and set up a standard;
publish, and conceal not . . .
I rejoice at thy word, as one that findeth great spoil.

                              —Jeremiah 50:2 and Psalm 119:162

I like a certain penumbra about your style
as opposed to mine—dull brilliance closing in
on mystery—dancing, losing at quadrille,
what you did this day or that or plan . . .

and your constitution (almanacs eclipsed
by bloody flux) with its central dark as if
halos are more important than the lapsed
leaping of a heart. When you are stiff

with words I see through, I like you and feel
for you—the tender grasp you never dare
to show, but do—and I would like to tell
the world you turned around one day and there

I was, opposing arms. I don't suppose
many one loves could embrace me as

seriously.

IV

That we may avoid connecting ourselves with the Politics of any
Nation, farther than shall be found necessary to regulate our own
trade; in order that commerce may be placed upon a stable footing
—our merchants know their rights—

What a free for all. I thought of you
rounding them up, conscripting, making them
sign and sing with good Yankee derring-do . . .

In Philadelphia the festering
blotched your dumb paper festivities—
no salvos bone fires no fan fares no firing . . .

The issues:
                    the issues were white lace to the whites
                    of their lies and red rags wagging for trade and blue
                    funks out of all of us—bloody fiscal frights—
                    the green ones not worth a sou . . .
I sew as I see

all that and following—my first design
to declare my own (if I ever paid
hard cash) independence— as I say to each
new flag as to my self:
                              I'll have it made.

V

*'Tis our true policy to steer clear of permanent alliances, ... let
those engagements be observed in their genuine sense. —But in my
opinion, it is unnecessary and would be unwise to extend them.*

To begin with, independence is a matter
of one's connections:
                        Uncle Ross, for instance,
noticed your lapsing lapel and fray of flounce,
brought my needle to your need, and your

charge to mine.
                        Ben saw the darkness split
and then he saw the light and we were free
of one former crudity.
                        You married money.
Let connections be ...
                        but ours—you broke it.

I did not offer trade to outerminglers
and keep no secret correspondences.
I don't accept your second thoughts. I guess
I know my rights. I can count on my fingers

and figure still. I have a genuine sense
of past affairs—what makes the present tense—

and I'll extend myself—what you forswear ...

VI

*That our Union may be lasting as time. —for while we are encircled
in one band we shall possess the strength of a Giant and there will
be none who can make us afraid—*

I was brought up on fairy tales, who wasn't?
   . . . I never saw a man so tall as you
   with buckles so silver and coat so blue . . .

Those "blind passions of princes" Diderot doesn't
trust, I trust—all tricked out and treatied.

   . . . I never saw a crown to crown your head
   except of airs, except when you saw red

at the thought of crowns. I never was so affrayed
as when your tattered tales grew serious.

   Giant come from lands where knights are white.
I guess Virginia is that sort, but out
   of place, I guess you have no home but this:

within
     the unlikely circle of
     thirteen I sewed for you—
             binding enough.

VII

And moreover, that we would guard against the Intrigues of any *and*
every foreign Nation who shall endeavor to intermingle (however
covertly and indirectly) in the internal concerns of our country—or
who shall attempt to prescribe rules for our policy with any other
power, if there be no infraction of our engagements with themselves,
as one of the greatest evils that can befall us as a people; for
whatever may be their professions, be assured fellow Citizens and
the event will (as it always has) invariably prove, that Nations as
well as individuals, act for their own benefit, and not for the benefit
of others, unless both interests happen to be assimilated (and when
that is the case there requires no contract to bind them together)—

Where did you learn to be so cynical,
dear George? Did I invariably prove my greed,
or what? Intrigue with me was not, after all,
arbitrary; you intermingled.

I'm not one of your "competitors in grimace"
that adorn high courts. My alliance is
covert, but free. I am your sweet red ace—
remember? —your trump of trade, to play as

you will. If I paint the cherry blue and net
all that's round and round to a lace and say
come-hither . . .
                so you think I only want to put
my hand in your pocket? I wish you could be
free. I will never grasp your grasp of treason,
but I want your trust, if not—anomaly—
your reason.

VIII

. . . so long as we profess to be Neutral, let our public conduct whatever our private affections may be, accord therewith. . . . A contrary practice is not only incompatible with our declarations, but is pregnant with mischief—embarrassing . . .

I never said a word—or spread about
anything more private than our trade
and how in the line of it I made
your specified flag.
                    How I feel about

it is something else; of the secrecy that for-
mality is the banner of, one says
nothing, but understands: one simply lays
aside one's foibles—
                    passion without form

that might explode the world. A white
swelling under the blue apron is tough
to lay aside however . . .
                    What is right

(about face turn about right and left face
turning red to turn about my trade
the way yours does . . .)
                    and what is left of us?

IX

That we may fulfill with the greatest exactitude all our engage-
ments: foreign and domestic, to the utmost of our abilities
whensoever, and in whatsoever manner they are pledged: for in
public, as in private life, I am persuaded that honesty will forever
be found to be the best policy.

Dear George—
            I lived on pins and needles—
                              George—
you lived on money like a man.
                        I held
you dear—remember that?
                  —and you withheld—
as only a man with holdings can—

                              the urge
to splurge.
            I thank you anyway
                              for giving
me the business—that made me,
                        so to speak,
first flagger (rah rah)
                  waver.
                              I bespeak
this union for my own—
                  designs are moving
even if not true.
                  Your precious cherry
parable sells a million—
                  I believe—

in telling things just so—
                        as make-believe
can make the honest man
                sterling.
                   Fancy
that freely then, my dear one—save
                    your own
face and forgive this note—
                                 the debt I'm in.
                                 Yours, Betsy

X

Thine eyes shall see the king in his beauty: they shall behold the
land that is very far off. —*Isaiah 33:17*

Broad and Wall—those obstacles so pain-
ful for a surveyor to get over—name
the corner turned to take your oath—in vain
remembering the plantations and the distant

dark beauties. You measured up and down
your Virginia magnitude and found it less
than in truth it was. The flag they wrap you up in
at last just might, just might, just fit you right.

O say I can see you one more time in your true
colors—purple and dusk and a good-bye green.
O say you can see me, taking my oath with you
to faithfully fulfill until farewell . . .

I'd make a dress for the ball—as politic
as not —to be— to love— too much to live

much past— this intersection in New York.

XI

In offering to you, my Countrymen, these counsels of an old and
affectionate friend, I dare not hope they will make the strong and
lasting impression, I could wish—that they will control the usual
current of the passions, . . . —But if I may even flatter myself that
they may be productive of some partial benefit, some occasional
good; . . . —this hope will be a full recompense for the solicitude
for your welfare, by which they have been dictated.

A so-so seamstress and a so-and-so
general do not make up a lasting piece
without some specific drawbacks.
                              And now,
and even then,
                    our independencies
established, many once-and-for-all-true
accounts lie strangely and—less so—hearsays . . .

and passions—
              yes the passions—
                            yes, they too . . .

and currents
              and counsels current . . .
                              I wish
I knew:
          what to make of any one, of you
and your separate wanting to be whole here

and there, of the trade and uncommon senses
between us . . .
                    I tried. Can free be never clear?

This began to be occasional . . .
Do you think there may be ever after, after all?

XII

*Had the situation of our public affairs continued to wear the same
aspect they assumed at the time the aforegoing address was drawn I
should not have taken the liberty of troubling you—my fellow
citizens—with any new sentiments or with a repetition, more in
detail, of those which are therein contained; but considerable
changes having taken place both at home and abroad, I shall ask
your indulgence while I express with more lively sensibility, the
following most ardent wishes of my heart.*

To say a flag unfurled is to say a man
of the world. (That's rhyming slang, but not less
true for its lack of sense.)
                                                The Rappahan-
nock (it means "the stream that comes and goes,"
like the money you most likely never threw
across it) keeps babbling the multiple false
and true tests
                        of the rumor and the rue
of all's fabric—
                        circulating cerise
that can purchase the right to speak of wrong
and flag it down, to tell where goodness lies

and nothing lasts for long, so long,
                                                so long . . .
easy come easy   to easy go lightly
                                        please . . .

The blood of revolution pools and mirrors
our blue moons, where blue ducks swim in pairs.

XIII

The history of our Revolution will be one continued lie from one
end to the other. The essence of the whole will be that Dr. Franklin's
electric rod smote the earth and out sprang General Washington.
That Franklin electrified him with his rod, and thenceforward these
two conducted all the policy negotiations, legislatures, and war.

—*John Adams*

Having wrung all the loose change out of
the laundry, having put my bottom rags
on the firing lines, having candied the last
cherries and baled all the hay sweet hay
a person could . . .

                I'm ready to snug down
where all the stories start.
                    I'm ready to sum
up—say life begins,
           then flags;
                embroidery
picks it up,
        now flags;
             then nothing, much.
Now, then: that's it.
            At last I'm off the on
and on
       and on the up and up
              and when

I reach the topple of all, should a single tatter
ripple down to earth, please put it under

a glass reflecting the oddly genuine
wince, upon our time.
                                    Tomorrow, then.

LESSON FROM THE COTTON MILLS
OF LOWELL

If it is said that many a one has here found a grave,
shall it not also be said that many a one has here
found the path to heaven?

—The Lowell Offering, *October, 1845*

I

Don't cry, Florilla, you know you aren't the first
to come homespun to Spindle City, find
yourself quite lost. The first day is the worst,
what with its solitude of ceaseless sound,
the overseer with his eye on you,
the trembling floor that hoggles all your bones;
you think that you will never learn to do
so much as doff a bobbin where time spins
round and round, unending snarl. I know
you miss Vermont, the quiet hills at dawn,
the farm, the family . . . Just think of how
your sacrifice will make it so your brother can
go to college. Meanwhile the mill will be
your school. You'll find yourself. You'll see.

II

The thunder, buzz and hiss and whiz, the whirr
of pulleys, rollers, spindles, flyers, wheels . . .
it's crickets, frogs and Jew's harps all together.
They are inside of me. I'm dragged by bells
from dawn 'til dusk. I am a single part
in one living machine, this work of threads
and circles, harness, hammer, springs. The heart

beats to the river ripping past and needs
nothing now but livelong friction. Still,
there's darkness in the loom, there is the lure
of madness, too, Tamar, a heaven-hell,
as voices weave themselves within the roar . . .
The mill rears high to the belfry; the sky is blood;
innumerable windows glitter, but the grounds . . . are mud.

III

Forget those darknesses, Florilla, think
of how bees gather honey from a poison flower,
and of our Sundays rambling, the mill-race bank,
wild roses tumbling, columbine clinging, where
we hear the bluebells ring . . . Those hours contain
our "alphabet of angels," meaningful
as our Improvement Circle where we learn
to speak as the city speaks and see the mill
as a moral lesson: how the whole world works
by singing clatter, where bells and threads converse
in a finished fabric, love. The mill-wheel's spokes
ceaselessly turn and drip, the hidden source
of everything. "The worm on the earth may look
up to the star." The circle, God's gravity, our work . . .

IV

A sin, Tamar? Where the spindles sing long yarns,
air steamed and windows shut, to think of Joan
whose work was menial, how while her arms
embraced a mindless service, she was alone
with unearthly messengers, her bonds undone
by hovering wings . . . They tell me that I am
the Gospel's handmaid as I weave . . . Eve span,

like me, from Genesis to Bethlehem . . .
Meanwhile, the lords of spade and shovel squat
in shanties and Hog Latin mucks the pure
syllables in my brain. On Merrimack Street
the devil's in needle books and ginger beer
and pavement Romeos. Joan burned for Charles
crowned. I hear you, angels, as my poor thread snarls

and I shall take my life and lay it down
in Pawtucket Falls, at the foot of the mill rearing high
to the belfry full of bats and the setting sun,
where the million windows glitter and speak to me.

MARIA MITCHELL (1818–1889)

I

Our female eyes are unsurpassed. Earth turns
civil through tiny stitches, seeds, pins, dust
tamed, shadow boxes, kitchen countings . . . Trust
me, this finicky eye toward Heaven discerns
well: nebulae, pearl-edged, and hazy Saturn's
tattings, lace fainter than spider webs. I keep
house now with my telescope. I sweep,
from one 'til dawn, the skies. My eye learns
which colors vary, which specks wander far
beyond our own ellipse. I trace the eclipse,
exact and spectral, seek "the interior
planet" behind the shadow tossed to earth.
From sun to sun . . . What good is work if it's
not infinite? I kneel at a creator's hearth.

II

Did I miss a man and children? Since you are
a woman, and kind enough not to be too shy
to ask a stranger, I will . . . I will try to answer.
I'm tired. This train's so slow. Now. What to say.
I've been so busy, always. Still, the sky
can be a cold companion; a short affair

Maria Mitchell, daughter of an astronomer, received, in 1847, the gold
medal offered by the King of Denmark for the first discovery of a tel-
escopic comet. In 1848, she was the first woman to be elected to the
American Academy of Arts and Sciences.

with a comet can leave one warm, but empty.
When you come home alone after the honor,
lionized, fêted, you can, quite suddenly,
want to put your arms around someone,
and there is nothing but the infinite
in your heart—no leap, no embrace. And then, the dawn
wipes out your closest friends. The northern lights
are fickle. The variable stars do not call out
for milk. I wonder . . . You, you tell me about it.

I HEARED DE ANGELS SINGIN':
HARRIET TUBMAN *for Arthur Brown*

Yes ma'am, de Almighty He make me
    dat kind of woman jump right up an' stand
      herself 'twixt some white devil man
an' dis poor bondman she know dat very day be set
    on his long run for it an' dat for to be
        free
an' I had a mind to join up wid him
      but den de Lord He see fit
      for to fix my head plumb where
de weight de white man hurl in wrath
    done hit an' it like to bust
      my skull an' de soul fly out.
Dey might to left me lay
    but I be worth cash money—
    strong critter like me—an' a load of sweat.
Master he let my mama nurse me gentle
    back from dat throb of dark
      an' ever since dat time
from out of dis hurted head de fits an' de visions
    come on me an' sure I be blessed
      to hear de angels sing, see 'cross dat line
to where my freedom life stretch out its hand.
        An' I be mighty blessed
           by anger too: when I thinks how *she* whip me
           for a mite of dust
           right out of de big house, how *he* loan me
           out to plow . . .

Times come dis heavenly power
    jus' come clean through me an' I knows for sure
      de Lord is in me to take my peoples through
      de tribulations of de railroad North

jus' like I do.
                    I got me eyes
for de dead of night an' ears
    for de leastest whispers.
                    I got me nerves
an' dey flitters like a snake's tongue,
    tick for to tell me
where de death-dangers be hidin' out.
                    It be like to de ways my papa knowed
                    to prophesy on weather.
                            I got me secret ways.

Den de times do come I jus' gets emptied out
    like to a rainbarrel sprung a leak.
        De air it go spirit-pale an' chill
            as a whipped child's heart
            an' I seems to fall
            down through some vast an' be landed in a sleep
nobody can't wake me from but de Lord Hisself
    when he goes to set dem angels singin'
        in dis hurted head of mine.

De good Lord He make me
    de kind of woman dreams
        de freedom dream:
                        I'm off an' arunnin' lost
                        an' aflyin' an' then I seems to see a line
                        an' on its other side be de greenest
                        fields wid lilies scripture-bright
                        an' womens robed all in white an' sun-gold
                        stretchin' out dere arms to me
an' I can't reach dem nohow
    'fore I falls, but dat don't keep me down
        when I be waked.
                    First time I runs off

myself all by my lonesome
I done heared about de so-called railroad
   to freedom
               but I didn't have no notions of whereabouts
               dem railroad tracks nor stations be.
So I jus' clinches my eyes
   to dat pillar of fire in de North of de nighttime sky
      an' cottons onto de use of belfries, corncribs,
      loads of coal, woodbins an' gulleys an' like dat.
I done pray
   an' limps my way along to liberty
      an' when I comes to cross
dat magic line at last, I feels dis fear,
   I looks hard at my poor hands
   to see if I be de same person,
a person on de far side, free.
A stranger in a strange land
   sure enough an' real soon I got me friends
      who knowed de railroad up an' down.
I got me work an' some cash money of my own
   an' dis thing freedom
   taste jus' fine as milk an' honey
             but I couldn't have me
no such thing widout thinkin' on all dem
   is still down slavin' in Maryland.
             So I saves
an' I asks an' I ponders de ways to go
   an' I sneaks back over
      dat magic line.

Nineteen times I makes dis journey down
   an' somewheres along de way
     I get me de name Moses
        an' de stories commence from dere
        can't nohow be true:

dey says how I might could part de waters
an' dry up swamps for my peoples to march on through,
how I might could lick a white slavecatcher
barehanded, smell dem devils out
two counties away, how I falls into my trance
for to speak wid de very angels
in de Celestial City
how I feeds my passengers
manna when de pickins is low
how when I'm 'bout to commence a raid
I'm like to turn
plumb invisible—
now dat be foolishness plain as day!
Truth be, I gets my orders from de Lord.
   An' O my passengers, all you close as kinfolk,
     you gives me de strength
along de way, fear-sweated, near sick wid hope
   an' showin' up so plain an' shabby runnin' low
   against de daybreak fields under de wild goose cries
  my chest is like to pain me
   from lovin'.
           Long as I done hears dem childrens cryin'
   knows dem old folks be listenin' for my song
I don't got me no choice.
   Even wid all dose bounty hunters prowlin' 'round
   an' wid ten thousand settin' on my poor head,
my callin' be to go down an' down again
   where I scouts out my place
   ripe for to be raided.
     Then sly as a cat in long grass I snugs me close
     by de Quarter an' commence my song:
       Who dat yonder all dressed in red?
       I heared de angels singin'.
       It look like de childrens Moses led,
       I heared de angels singin'.

Never a one make a move but I knows dey knows
   an' dere hearts be turnin' yonder
      towards de praise-grove
         where each alone come sneakin'
         an' each come alone all roundabout
to hark for de whippoorwill in de dark
      dark as blackstrap; an' dark dere lonesome shadows
      kneelin' down 'twixt dem stones
         tiltin' all whichways over de restin' souls
         we be leavin' behind.
I whistles out the whippoorwill again
      an' dey be all gatherin' round an shiverin'
      an' Canada seem 'bout as far as Heaven.

Well, I runs dem off,
      de baby be drugged wid laudanum,
      de old man upholded by de young.
Numb like to sleepwalkers, nerved-up or notional,
      each grabbin' to each in de dark for to keep
         us one whiles
         keyed on stars
I leads us in zigzags, backtracks, bids dem keep
      dere faces shut so I might can cock my ear
         to de white whoops an' de thumpin' of dem hooves
         be death to us, an' de killer dogs snifflin'
         through leaves by de banks of brackish water
            we slushes our feets through for to put dem off
            for jus' a little ways . . .
Bad off by dawn we be hunkered down
      in some wet ditch done prickled by de rough
      pine boughs we lays like a blessin' over us.
Come nigh dusk, an' if my heart beat safe
      I creeps out as I knows traps and scavengin'.
         I finds us maybe a windfall
         old walnuts, some moldy cobs

lyin' round in de tumbled stalks
or it comes to pass de Lord give me
to catch us a woodchuck or squirrel.

So we plods an' crawls an' plods—
    it be one long day of nights.
        De brambles go snatch an' de branches swats
        an' de ground open up all sudden-like
        to catch our stumblin' feets . . .
An' den some times
    my passengers gets dis doubt an' queasy hungerlook
    deep down dere eyes . . .
"Where we be, Moses?"
    an' dey be like to cuss me.
"Somewheres in Creation, on our way,"
    I says an' I knows
        in my bones dey be like to commence a ruction
            be like to call down de horsemens
            'pon us wheres we be hid.
I takes my stand den, I stands up
    to dem doubters.
                    "You been worse off," I says,
                    "you been bondfolk.
Jus' lean on me
    we got us a covenant,
jus' hold to me a little ways
    an' fore de sun be up
        we be like to come to one of de Lord's
        best-connected stations—dey be Quaker folks—
                    won't no patrollers catch us
                    under dat dere barn floor
                    an' we might can have us some milk
                    an' maybe apples . . ."

. . . And blessed be Levi Coffin an' Gerrit Smith
an' Thomas Garrett—two thousand souls passed through

his hands on de way to freedom—God bless dem all.
An' blessed be Frederick Douglass an' good John Brown.
    ('Fore I ever meets dat man de Lord show me a vision
    where de serpent eats him up.)
                          O, yes,
I seen de sacrifice a-comin', I witnesses
de tribulations, de abominations, de lamentations,
    de mighty war, O, yes,
but I sees dem womens arrayed in glory
    jus' as clear
    an' I sees de livin' womens—
        I shakes Miss Alcott's hand
            in Concord an' de folks be gatherin' round
            for to help us on our way.
I sees de seals set on dere foreheads
    as dey raise up dere voice.

I never learned me to read nor write
    but I ain't like to disremember
    a single thing what come to pass
in de deeds of my life dat de Lord be pleased
    to give unto me.
                I done my best.
I be a messenger, a conductor of souls
    to liberty.
An' I nurses dem wounded Union mens
    wid potions my mam's mama teached her to fix
    from roots an' leaves.
I washes so many wounds one day
    I be washin' blood wid thinner blood
        'til I thinks I be washin' all dem in de blood
        of de Lamb where de bloods all do mix.
        Praise Him.

An' now what be happenin'
    is my friends is gettin' after dem high hats

down at Washington, askin' what dey gonna do
    for dis old woman done so much.
I don't say nothin'.
No ma'am, noways. I be recompensed
    by soul-riches, by de listenin' of all dese strangers
    comes to me—what once be bondfolk
    well as dose ain't never been—
        in dis strange land.
Dey comes together.
    Ain't strangers no more.
Dey comes to me for to hear de mysterious ways,
    for to hear my storytellin', for to be a-singin':
        Who dat yonder all dressed in blue?
        I heared de angels singin'.
        It look like de childrens jus' come through,
        I heared de angels singin'.
"Where we be now, Moses?"
    An' I answers slow,
        "Don't you worry you none.
It be a long ways to go yet,
    here ain't no Heaven
        but we be somewheres in Creation
            on our way."

CONCORD'S CHILD:
LOUISA MAY ALCOTT

Do you want to know the real Louisa May?
Does one exist? Right now she's folding pink
flannel penwipes in the hospital
where Dr. Rhoda Lawrence oversees
her naps and drops, massage and baths. My bones
throb, my right thumb's paralyzed for good
from pressing down on moral pap, my voice
is froggy, all the hurts I've ever had,
the vertigo, dyspepsia, rheumatic pains,
come back in force. I shiver in my furs
and rummage in the wonder of my life . . .

Everything must have its meaning in the end,
if only I can re-arrange . . . (that's all
my fiction does, it fixes times and smiles,
transforms real griefs and faults). I need to search
my diaries, my letters. I destroy
and add, but what's the use—the truth is still
unsayable. One story of my life
was started as "Success"; it ends as *Work*,
and as in *Little Women*, something's lost.
Is it the mysterious key, the one that springs
the vortex in my brain where duchesses,
evil-hearted actresses, grandees,
banditti, nuns, sylphs, orphans, suicides,
opium eaters, artists, wretches, all
the elements of temperament, release
the plots and counterplots behind a mask
worn to please?
                    Oh, Papa, let me please
you; Marmee, let me follow all the steps
to Concord's transcendental home, if not

to your Celestial City. I admit
impatience, selfishness and willfulness,
independence, vanity and pride,
not to mention love of cats—it's here
in this old diary from Fruitlands days.
Dressed in linen, scrubbing, grubbing, crowded
by visiting idealists, dubious,
we eat our pure and bloodless solar meals
of water, graham bread, apples, wholesome nuts,
gossiping of gross Brook Farm. It's hard
to be the daughter of experiments,
take cold baths and keep a diary
for inspection, nod through clouds of talk
of moral kingdoms, Edens, Genius . . .
There we are with our bust of Socrates
and Papa's visions of consociative life,
"the Newness," the infinity of man,
the perfect life where "outward abstinence"
means "inner fullness."

                    Oh, I tried, but still
I was hungry, I craved privacy.
Dark, demonic, no child of my father's light,
somehow a freak, a girl-boy, wild and queer,
born carnivore with lurid tendencies,
I dreamed of a gigantic love . . . How could
I translate misery to goodness, then?

I wander through that life, imagine it,
spin crazy webs to catch the moments in
no particular order, stages here
and there, and now and then, lights up,
down, up, the curtains, costumes, words
my own and not my own . . .

                    There was that dream—
randomly recalled—from Switzerland
where I'd been whirling in the grandest tour,

whirling so far as poverty permits,
and yet some part of the brain would lead me home
to Concord. I dreamed that I returned alone.
I looked for Orchard House, dear Apple Slump,
but there was a great gray castle there instead,
stone, with towers and arches, antique bridge . . .
No one knew me. A stranger said he sold
the place to Mr. Alcott for a school.
And where did Mr. Alcott get the means?
"From his daughter, it seems, the one who died
ten years ago." I know then I am dead.
Dead, I watch boy-children run around
the grounds with Father, young and brown and plump.
I nod to him, but he can't recognize . . .
I catch myself in a mirror, all fat and gray;
quietly I go away.
                              Awake,
I feel betrayed. I've never lost that pang.
I don't know why. Inside of us it seems
we carry these betrayals, many such;
we keep the secret end in sight and write
to multiply the possibilities
inside, outside . . . I never dreamed I'd play
so many parts, betray so many lives:
chambermaid and doll dressmaker; nurse
"Tribulation Periwinkle" in
a ballroom full of death beds, tending wounds
in ghastly air until her own lungs break;
"Flora Fairfield" writing moral scraps
and "A. M. Barnard" bringing in the cash
with tales Louisa Alcott could not sign . . .
And one of me is rich, one destitute,
one staid, one reckless, one anonymous
in passion's vortex, one is named "Aunt Jo,"
grown up tomboy, topsy-turvy still;
good Rose and earnest Christie, plus those boys

made up of ones I might have been or loved;
and Sylvia, a subject of her moods,
in love with one who's doomed to die . . . but who
can truly love without the end in sight?

Mostly the dead preside in Concord now:
Mr. Hawthorne, mysterious and shy,
pacing past Orchard House with all his ghosts;
and Mr. Emerson, to whom I wrote
all those unsent letters, to whose Goethe
I played Bettina, leaving sheafs of flowers
on his next-door stoop; and Margaret Fuller draped
in Grecian folds for conversation's sake;
Theodore Parker with his rolling voice;
and most of all . . . but how can I speak of him?
I must. (I dreamed of a gigantic love.)
Homely, manly Henry, shaggy, gruff
and tender to the child I was—what eyes
he had! With him I saw the tanager
set the woods on fire and heard the wood
thrush speak philosophies of golden rod.
We spotted Indian arrowheads, otter's tracks,
found high bush blueberries, prunella flowers,
tickled the lizard, rowed on Walden Pond . . .
Some called his silence rude, some said he ate
asparagus from the "wrong" end. (I ask which
is that?) I thought his bluntness honesty,
even his coldness excited me. Gloomed eyes
under his old straw hat, his shoulders broad
under the old checked shirt, he let me touch
his flute and raise his spyglass to my eye.
With jackknife, twine, he could build anything.
I lost him when I ceased to be a child.
(It was no secret women tired him out.)
Before I took myself to Washington

to nurse our Union boys and learn firsthand
the male anatomy, Thoreau was dead.

Papa, my life has paid your debts, my hand
now smooths the white hairs on your head, my pen,
although it refused to write your life, the cost
of living for Idea's sake, moves now
according to your will, your dream, your faith
in "American Genius" . . . If you'd had a son . . .
I did my best, no genius, it's true,
but as a pilgrim I made progress, showed
the world the American Home, told
the heart of my heritage. I did my best . . .

I wanted to make sunshine for everyone,
always. Marmee—you taught me that and when
I put the Alcott family bound in cloth
into your Christmas stocking—I knew you knew.
You even loved my "Mephistopheles"
published without my name. You understood
my *Moods.* When I came home from Washington
to a house that seemed to have no roof, a house
where no one knew me in my delirium,
you let my fury be. My room was full
of men and one, a wicked Spanish duke
in velvet, black, my spouse, stood over me,
leapt from closets, in at windows . . . I
appealed to the Pope in imaginary Latin,
was burnt as a witch and went to a boring Heaven,
but you brought me back as you've always brought me back
to myself—ungothic Louy, daughter, loved.

Certain things a life cannot contain.
Uncertain things it can. I know I've played
a certain moral hand for all its worth,

but somehow that's outside, outside of *me*.
And blood and thunder—that's outside me too.

Clocks and smiles and smiles and clocks—now why
do those words come to me as summary?
I have found time for everything and smiled
my way through poverty and gala teas,
oversoul and oysters, John Brown hanged,
Van Ambergh's New Great Golden Menagerie,
the telltale mist that rose from Lizzie's corpse,
playing Mrs. Jarley on the stage,
the little women at Vassar tearing lace
from my gown for keepsakes, Mrs. Bliss
and her magnetic trances, Boston burned,
Flower Fables, women's causes, May's
death, Marmee's, May's child in my arms,
Mr. Emerson's barn and the summerhouse
of willow wands, picnics at "Spiderland,"
that bridesmaid's dress that seemed sackcloth and ashes,
the Polish boy who hated the Russian baron
while I hated the Virginia colonel at Vevey,
being revolutionary and
American, certainly . . .
                                        broken clocks
and broken smiles, the wonder of a life
when everything speeds together at the end.

Any moment I expect to hear
of Papa's passing. Once he told me: act
just as if each day were someone else's
birthday. We've shared our birthday ever since
the day I was born. It's hard to realize
that I am I, and my parents coincidence . . .
Papa said, and I never understood,
"Life is the dispersion of the identities

and the concentration of the diversities."
Now that makes me smile—how he'd prance through time
and space with his cronies, fly right out of sight,
a Platonic balloon. What is my passion for
roses compared to that? (Oh, Rose, my deadly
good Victorian princess, how you bloom!)

Have I made parables where none exist?
Have I left the difficult passions out?
Have I repeated myself and worn a mask
not even I could see through? Life is still
a puzzle to me, more mysterious
as I go on. There's always a task undone,
a word left out . . .
                    A child comes to the door
of Orchard House and mourns: "I thought you would
be beautiful." I can't be everything.

I'm tired of fussing over this skeleton
and all the bits and pieces of a life
randomly recalled—to myself alone.
I live on gluten gruel now, gems and cream.
My father wears my glasses instead of his
and sometimes knows me, sometimes not, like me.
I smile. My sister's daughter comes to me
for a story and I spin something out
of Concord's childhood, thinking of the bird
that set the woods on fire, the flowers that spoke,
and even while my lips are moving, I
watch the shadow lengthen by my chair.

THE BANDIT QUEEN REMEMBERS

for Robert Taylor, Jr.

Of all women of the Cleopatra type, since the days of the Egyptian queen herself, the universe has produced none more remarkable than Bella Starr, the Bandit Queen. Her character was a combination of the very worst as well as some of the very best traits of her sex. She was more amorous than Anthony's mistress; more relentless than Pharaoh's daughter, and braver than Joan of Arc. Of her it may well be said that Mother Nature was indulging in one of her rarest freaks, when she produced such a novel specimen of womankind. Bella was not only well educated, but gifted with uncommon musical and literary talents, which were almost thrown away through the bias of her nomadic and lawless disposition, which early isolated her from civilized life, except at intervals, when in a strange country, and under an assumed name, she brightened the social circle for a week or a month, and then was, perhaps, lost forever.

From *Bella Starr, the Bandit Queen, or the Female Jesse James,* Richard K. Fox Publications, 1889.

beginnin a letter for my daughter, 1888

It's quieter 'n a wood pussy walkin on the moonlight
at Younger's Bend without you Pearl
and all my ruffian moochers are either on the scout
somewheres else or out gatherin critters
and your poor dumb brother run out as I took the quirt to him
pretty fierce for that Catoosa catawampus
him riskin bein reduced to nothin but a cottonwood blossom
and after all his leather-bodied mother
has done by way of caution. I get my share of swag
but I don't tease no serious arms
plus I don't like him turnin my best mare to a nag
with a cold jaw. But now that's enough
about Eddie, nothin but a hopeless son of that hopeless
gun Jim Reed.
              You now, my Pearl,
you are the daughter of Cole Younger who was and is
even if he is locked up in Stillwater
one of the legends we couldn't live without, and me.
Sometimes I reckon you are forgettin
just who you are and just who you are supposed to be.
Pearl Younger there ain't a single other
soul I ever had any hopes for save yours. I gave you
a name to live up to and gave you
lessons in how to be a lady and lessons how not to
serve out your time as some common
brainless calico. Now I don't know what you figure

you are doin with that bastard baby
of yours runnin away from home but you had just better
think again, my Pearl, and remember
just where you come from and say over your mother's name
and ponder how she has to live with it.

a note to attach to that newspaper hooey

Pearl, Baby, there's just no tellin
what those tinhorn medicine tongues augurin
in the *Police Gazette* and all tangled up in their own
flannelmouth yarns will cook up concernin
yours truly or the "Bandit Queen"
as one has kindly christened me
when she finally lays 'em down.
I guess I'd be bored as a geldin in green-up time
if they didn't lift a pen to take a squirt at me
seein how much they muck about to enhance
Jesse and Frank and other dangerous men
I can wrap right around my pinkie easy
as a cowhand bindin the feet of a split tongue dogie.
But ever since the hangin judge
sent me and Sam Starr up to Pandemonium to weave
cane chair bottoms and split rock it's only Sam
that's had to go on the dodge
and my part's mostly gossip.
You don't have to believe your old Ma
is straighter 'n a wagon tongue, mind you,
as this child has been known to tell a tale
tall as a steeplejack's pocket,
but here I am aimin for mostly true

chin music to remind you, Pearl, that
even if I'm full of fool's words
it's not fool's gold I'm ever aimin for
and the heart in it is honester
than that Texas butter that is mostly lard.

remindin her how it wasn't easy even then

Fatman Parker ain't the only judge in my life.
Your grandpa was called "Judge" back in Carthage, Missouri,
where he kept sweet liquors, a civilized kitchen and wife,
beds and straw for rent and Ozark type flattery
for hooligans goin to Texas as we one day would with all
the bloody Quantrill stuff behind us.
                                   I used to dream
an Osage warrior might anytime crash our zigzag and steal
me away, first scalpin the "Judge" and Ma. I'd dream
they'd make me their daughter in war paint and savvy.
Or else maybe one of Quantrill's men would spot me ridin so fast
my shadow couldn't catch up. Then I'd leave the Female Academy
to be a real Bushwhacker, not just my brother's last
resort for scout. I'd smile and wink and spy my way
right into the Yankee ranks and leave them wonderin how
as they died.
                    The closest I ever got to that—listen—I
know I've told it a million times, but Pearl, it's different now
you're grown with a woman's understandin of your own:

When I was scoutin and nosed out how the Jayhawk Yankees
were goin to drygulch my best brother Bud for his blood
revenges, and they caught me and ran me in to Judge Ritchery's,
I didn't just charm the lot by poundin out a gallopade

on his piano and I didn't just cut them cherry branches
as I left for horse speed. I gave that burblin monster
just what he asked for in his privatest chambers.

You might say that was the day my spirit put my body on
ice, thin ice, like the November slick on a pond
you see your face skim over as you're fallin in.

a word about power plus a second thought

Just because I knew my power as a woman, Pearl,
I didn't stop with that. Even before Bud was chilled
I learned to ride with my knees, jump up the dust
and iron out the kinks in a green cull's back.
I practiced slappin leather in the barn till I could
hit a pheasant's eye from across a field.
By the time we had to vanish to Texas I could
fork a horse and haul off and make smoke
so as to make any man shiver. I'd see them ring-tailed
roarers at the bar like steers makin merry-go-round
in high water, mud in their eyes and like
to die for nothin, and I'd laugh because with a quick
change of duds and saddle I could
bring them to drool like pigs in a peach orchard.
Just because I knew my power as a woman, Pearl.

Now you, you never had to prove yourself enough.
I didn't want you to have to go the same route I did,
in order to be wanted, the way I wanted wanted men,
but I didn't want you to go all soft and stupid.
The world is never going to give you what you need.
Is it too late to tell you that? I take up my pen
now, if it isn't, to tell you, and that goes for love.

yet another unanswered letter

Maybe a gal needs only one background to lean
against and not fall down. I've tried to give you two.
Lean too far one way, you got to stick out your legs and run.
Stand up too straight and still, someone will scythe you.

When you were learnin to walk, Rosie, I used to laugh
to see you totter and reach for pants legs under
the poker tables. That's over. Now I am sayin enough
is enough. Hang on. Climb up if you can. Plunder.

But don't be lettin them hook their bootheels on your bed.
That's low, Pearl, that's lower than I've ever been.

Come home to me, Pearl. I'd rather you be dead
than on Front Street. Don't go tellin me it's what I've done.

remindin her how I met up with Cole

Texas was full of badmen full of brag and fight
pirootin around them bluffs and yucca between
honey mesquite and dog towns, former choir boys
and ex-deputies on the owl-hoot trail who might
just turn out to be legends. One night a man
called Jesse James came hallooin up to our dugout
hearin we was from Missouri, and with him, hale
as hard money, the brothers Younger, plus Jim Reed,
and all of 'em grinnin like skunks eatin garlic
to think of the Ozark blood buzz we were like
to share, along with some common doins. But my Ma,

who never gave me a thing but her bent for headaches
said she wouldn't do for punks, so that left me
to cook up a mess of dough-gob and sop and break
out a can of love apples and flutter my eye,
'specially at Cole Younger, him smooth as rattlesnake
root with its milky ooze and his tall moonrise smile,
so blond and so slow . . . I simply took to him
like honeysuckle to fencin, like it does to bloom.

and what happened after that

So it's not that I don't remember, Pearl,
what a sudden case of spoons is like, it's that
it just doesn't last that's all.
And it wasn't all sparkin in the moonlight
loungin with your daddy-to-be whisperin in my ear
I was pretty as a heart flush him lyin there
handsome as an ace-full on kings but
that is how it started out.
Deep down I knew he had about as much use
for me as a hog for a ruffled shirt,
thinkin my main talent was for applesauce.
Then he didn't like the looks of me knocked up—
sound familiar?—and started preachin like the sinbuster
he was in his faithless dreams—poor Cole, King Cole—
he high-tailed it out of Texas quotin chapter
and verse and then in Liberty, Missouri,
and thereby hangs a tale,
him and Jesse invented bank robbery
American style.
In '66 it was and smack on Valentine's Day.

rememberin how she turned belly-up

So what if the bluebirds were back and the new
crops of rabbits snufflin under the fuzzy hawbushes
and the bees fiddlin and pokin in the wild plum . . .
that sure ain't no excuse, Pearl!

That moon-calf breed of yours now—poor as a coot
naked almost as a worm and whiffy on his lee side
no more savvy than a snake has hips and no mounts
and no plans to sugar-coat you.

You were brought up for pure clover, my Pearl,
not for castin yourself at a swine and a life
of tough pickins and needles and a mess of sprouts.
That's why I packed you off to Chickalah.

So then the crows were fattenin and the umpteenth
crop of rabbits snufflin . . . very next thing I know—
hearin it from a neighbor first—you're all peakish
and undeniably caught with the goods.

I couldn't stomach no blasted event that's why
I went lickety-zip out and found you a livery-man
who'd pay the vet to clean you out and still was willin
to marry. Then you had to go jump the gun

and ankle off to Arkansas to have your bastard leavin me
feelin just like I did when you died behind the lights
in Dallas in the middle of your song—empty empty handed
with the dowry I might have . . . might have . . .

So now you've got your booby prize, Cole's daughter,
and what have I got? I swear I never yet blotted out
a member, but if I find the galoot did this I will
make him worm food at a hand gallop

scatter him like a dose of the wind.

maybe sayin I'm not all that hard

But if I named you for any one reason, Pearl,
it was for the perfection of our romance
the pale moonrise and shine around the telltale
speck of grit left behind, a coincidence
hard and soft at once to touch. But, Pearl,

perfection isn't meant to be repeated, Pearl.
You were to be an end in yourself to me
and to yourself someday to be the crownin jewel
no one could steal and what I could never be
after my disgrace. I chose to have you, Pearl.

I didn't want you to be ordinary, Pearl.
An ordinary woman is like a box canyon
with one entry and only one exit from herself.
But perfection never leaves any way so open.
I was ambushed in my one way, Pearl.

That glamour time in Dallas even with my pearl-
handled pistols and got up in silk and velvet
for dealin to rustlers holed up in that hotel
makin our livin with poker and faro and roulette
even with you right by my side, sweet, Pearl . . .

our first Dallas spree continued and ended

We had pretty near all we needed didn't we, Rosie?
I was keepin you safe and supplyin our livery stable
and fancy doins. Everybody knew I had my Pearl.

No one touched you knowin how I was trigger-happy
till Pa got wind of some fiddlefaddle concernin me
and stole you right out of your crib in Planter's Hotel
while I was busy down below and with nothin carnal.

So I lit right out for Scyene to get back my baby.

That's when Pa locked me in my room just like he could up
and save me for a proper motherhood and meanwhile
you were grisslin away and Ma was whinin somethin awful
and I was thinkin how I told Jim I smelled a trap
and hopin he might figure out some gallant way to come
get us out of the mess. It was pandemonium.

Seemed like dark ages hollerin how I was ready to cash in
and take my place with the angels rather 'n play canary
in my home sweet home—guess they figured they'd marry
me to some sodbuster and make me hillbilly decent again.

Ha! I'd got hold of a bread knife halfway fixin on carvin
up my wrists and let the ruby run out where they'd see
when I hear that ping on the window and damn me
if Jim Reed isn't climbin up quiet as a rat in a grain bin

with a brandin iron to pry me out and he is grinnin
like a stuffed possum. So I start stompin like a mockey
to hide the racket of crackin wood and before you can say
Goodbye Old Paint I'm Leavin Cheyenne

I'm slidin down the sods and skurtlin through the panic grass
and leavin you, Pearl, with what I can't still choose.

not advisin that this is the proper way

Turns out the whole Fischer gang is out there
in the dark darker 'n the inside of a wolf's gut
with even the horses on tiptoes and about to let out
the biggest laugh this side of the Cimmaron. The men are
moon-gazin at no moon through the neck of their bottle
and I almost have a second thought about my life as I fall
astride a saddle and we all take off like the clatter
wheels of hell shootin in the air, the foxed judge rampagin
on his back porch and with his rusty hog leg jammed,
my gang-in-waitin goin crazy as popcorn on a hot stove,
seein double and feelin single all. I hang on and damn
the judge and this and that and you and myself and love
and then Jim Reed announces we would have the weddin.

So Fischer gets out his Bible II, the outlaw's who's who,
black as a witchcat's overcoat, and solemnly slur-preaches
what to-do marriage is and they wait for me to say I do,
and I do with my mare's flanks heavin as Jim reaches
for my reins and hollers "Ditto!" And so it was done.
That night I married the lot, not one, to be left alone.

remindin her again of the consequences

After that weddin on horseback and all the palaver
about it it didn't take much for Texas to be closin in
on the identity of Jim Reed who when it came to rustlin
had about as much brains as a tin pan has fur.

So we headed for Jim's folks in Rich Hill, Missouri.
I got knocked up and was poorly so Jim went off wranglesome
and crawled the hump of a man. I couldn't help him.
On the dodge he was bunglin robbery plain and fancy.

Then he'd creep home dauncy and sometimes with some pal
on the scout with him, dead bored and chompin their bits
to pieces, like me. One time he brought home this
Cherokee called Sam Starr, six foot five inches tall

who was smilin like a jackass in a haystack.
I dropped my needle.
He was fresh as a breeze of the Territory, Pearl,
with a whiff of blood-revenges, a whiff of maniac.

A marriage even a fake one should be more, my Pearl,
than cipherin the blind trails to one hideout after another.
I might as well have been a bounty hunter.
Did you miss me in Scyene? You were still so small.

remindin her how I did come back to her

It wasn't much fun bein stuck out in California
with word out the James gang was there and the banks

sittin with their knees together like virgins.
I was saltier than Lot's wife and Jim was jumpy
as a frog in a skillet and even baby Eddie seemed like
he was on the prod and hankerin for a Texas type
no-questions-asked rendezvous.
                          So back we trekked
about a million miles of drag dust and bad graze
tumbleweed and all-thorn till even my milk was gyppy
all the time tastin Dallas scamper juice in our dreams
figurin how we'd drop by Scyene and get set up
at Pa's brand-artist hideout by pleadin for the baby
and gettin you back, Pearl.
                          I was plenty afraid
you'd have forgot me, Rosie, so it was like a pardon
to a lifer when you ran out to swing from my stirrup
pricklin at least my Ma's heart.
                          Even though the judge
was still techy as a peeled snake seein Jim Reed
and threatenin to comb Jim's hair with his six-gun
with Jim offerin the judge a halo gratis . . .
                          But I guess they struck
some sort of Ozark bargain while I was off gatherin
my brains and charms together.
                          And for a mighty good reason:
Lo! there is Jesse himself slouchin at the bar
paintin his tonsils, so I ooze over slow and polite
as pooch and ask him how's crops and rib him up some
till he asks am I lookin for a tie-in.
                          That's how come
Jim went hootin off all happy for Gadshill and I
got left behind as usual.
                          But I had you, Baby.

two jobs I take a little credit for

I was thinkin maybe Jim could strike it rich
and then come join my shady horse business in Dallas.
But he was ridin willows most of those bad days
holin up in bloody Starr country not makin scratch.

Meanwhile I was gettin connected, nights pretty much
taken with dealin. I plain refused to go and keep house
for Cole's outfit. I was captivatin and bridle-wise,
a right fine pianist and sneaky, but still had this itch

to ride astride and masked and stand up a stage
for the hell of it. It is me plans that ambush
between Austin and San Antonio where Cole is Jack
and Jim is Bill and I am Rosa. The men take gold watches
and cash and I go riflin through the sack of mail.
I swear the love letters are the best of all the swag.

But that doesn't mean I'm soft. Oh no. When after that
Jim got a bag on his head and went off with that man—
Wilder or Dickens or Morris—who's supposed to be on the scout
with him—we used to change names easy as a kitten
jumps over a caterpillar—
                          and when that Judas shoots him
they call me as the widow to identify the body

that happens to be left in the sun to cook in its own slime.
Well, I ain't about to let a Judas collect the bounty.

I am not a woman who cries.
I say I am sorry, Gentlemen.
This is not the body of Jim Reed.
I say you are mistaken.

I left the mistake to be finally buried.
Jim Reed was one of the littler guys.

here I just want her to know

Dear Pearl, how I wanted you.
I didn't send you off like I sent your brother
because I knew what Ma would do
in the mistaken interest of making her daughter
all over again. I knew her,
the darks of her, her rooms too well. I wanted
you to hanker after more . . .
Hell, Pearl, that's sentiment. I flaunted
you on your peacherino
pony and swelled myself up like a carbuncle
to have you sing and dance so
the Dallas stage would clamor: She belongs to Belle.

How was I to know your poor brain would burst
under the limelight? That night was the worst.

how sorry it made me

Worse than when Cole went off hell-raisin and I
had to explain the father of you.
Worse than seein Jim as free lunch for a coyote.

What's a little girl to do
when the moon comes up like a dinner plate—
serve son-of-a-bitch stew
and mew? Calico around, a spur gaffin her gut?

In Carthage I used to
sit my brother's saddle and it felt just fine.

There are just two
ways: the gun and the piece of lace, to get your own,
to make them dance.
Pearl, do you recall how them hotshots danced you over
the hotel tables of chance
as I was dealin, callin you Lady Luck? Then quicker

'n Hell could scorch the plume in my Stetson, you
fell down, lance of my pride, as if on cue.

seein this heap of writin on my table

I fixed on givin you the straight tips, my Rosie,
all this paper I stained for you—and now it's all
comin back to me unopened . . .
                              I can't figure why
I allowed they'd catch up with you . . .
                                    you with Cole

Younger's blood in you and with Jim Reed's folks
providin shelter and then there was all you heard Sam tell
about the lines and lyin low.
                              Quandary talks
ballyhoo to itself like hope—
                              I say, Dear Pearl,—
might as well say Dear Me—
                              Here is our one-way memoir
about as close as an oyster.
                              Your bastard girl
forces you, rapes from inside . . .
                              No pigsticker
pokes deeper to split the carcass.
                              Child,
with you sendin me back to me still sealed . . .

what they call the missin years

If only you knew, Pearl, how many the mornin
with a head too big to crowd into a corral
and breath to crack a mirror, I woke up missin—
a hole in me huge as robber's cave—
could you have stayed invisible?

With desert rats and wish-book breeds,
river snipers, gamblers in and out of the sacks,
in and out with suck-egg dogs and crowbait playin
faro and piano and wicked and sweet
together, I'd wake up and be missin . . .

the lady you were supposed to be turnin into, her mask,
her only mask female and marriage her only risk.

but continuin the letters anyhow

There was the spell it was gettin pretty hot
around Blue Duck and Jim French and the Pinkertons
near to saltin the Spaniard's tail.
Then I was the brain and wits for a good many
and knowin the finer things in a clandestine
life when I wasn't fancy dressin down in Fort Smith
prancin like a cat on mud and arrangin everyone's bail
and defense—it made me chipper as a coopful of catbirds, too,
as all the great seizer ever had on me was circumstantial
with me in my widow's weeds and elusive as a ground cuckoo.
Got in one real mess for burnin down that boomtown shanty
with Emma Jones that harumscarum bit with her tongue waglin
like some weanlin but I still had my looks and before you could say
Helldorado, I managed to borrow more 'n enough from a fat greenhorn
in catalogue togs and fofarraw. Then in another place
I went on some high toots with the wildcat's child Jane
from Deadwood when she was not hangin round that circus
prince of pistoleers of hers. Showed me her knack for cadgin
drinks and then we'd go whoopin down some main street
shootin out the lights and pretendin we were a couple of blah-zay
cow hunters come to see the elephants. After that
I might have to resort to whisperin sweet nothins to a turnkey
or sharin a little tangle-leg with some ex-con tin star.
Then I'd get the gossip like how Cole up in Minnesota
got nabbed in a bank job so I finally cut loose with Sam Starr
and we did so very fine I guessed I'd settle for etcetera
with him and make a nest for my kids and develop my talent
for arrangin things across borders and general management.
I married corrals for beef on hoof and caves for hidin and I am
still here with nothin on me but circumstantial evidence I am
even alive.

comin to the Starr country

You never met old Tom Starr, Pearl, kind
as a Death Valley buzzard, face like hammered mud.
But he was wise in his murderous ways
as a tree full of owls, and he could talk the hind
legs off a donkey. Well, I just poured out my eyes
on him like blackstrap on a rotten log and he'd
let his old pemmican tongue hang out and give me
all I needed to know about the Cherokee snickersnee.

Then there was Sam, gritty as eggs rolled in sand
but pleased with me as a bear cub with honeycomb.
I guess I wasn't no grass widow looking for a rake
but I liked the idea of Starr, of havin my name
ring like instant legend, of eighty acres of land,
a place to stash my Pearl, a place for hide-and-seek.

some little morals from Dodge City

Look at it this way, Pearl: I'm in the business
of showin people what they really hanker after.

I loaned Blue Duck two grand with him lookin motherless
ears aflop like a tick-fevered dogie and in an hour
this pack of culls cleans him down to his spurs.
So I go in and I see they've got enough paper money
to burn a wet mule. I got the drop and I curse
and while they're gapin like goosed women Blue Duck and me
depart poco pronto. Still I told those drunks they could
come and get their change some time and if they see fit to

I'll sure give it to them. I respect a yack on the prod
for a reason. I'd even risk a visit to the hoosegow

to have them think what this child is riskin after all.
      It's bein a saint is anti-social.

remindin her how Younger's Bend is her place

I guess you'll forgive me, Pearl, if I try to scribble out
some rhymes. They ain't Byron like I used to read you
but it takes my mind off . . . and whenever it's quiet
like it is tonight . . . but tonight I feel more freehand
like I used to draw in school when we were supposed to trace
and I'll pretend that maybe you are goin to read this one.
Remember how I fetched you and Eddie, darlin, after Cole
leaked out of the landscape into Stillwater? Remember
comin up the windin trail from the river through scrub oak
and locust and hawbushes so thick a bird could hardly turn
itself around to build? You feared Sam Starr at first
with his plucked eyelashes and his high lonesomes,
his wily, crooked smiles. But it was for you, Baby,
I married this land. It was to hide you, my treasure,
under Hi-Early mountain and see you grow with the wild grape
and roses and make dolls from the walnut and red velvet
sumac, cuddle you deep between boulders, persimmon and sycamore.
And it was for you I named it.
Remember how you learned to entertain on that old piano
got with the boot from Ogalala—first job Sam and I
pulled off together—and you didn't mind the jolly company
did you, Baby? All those cow nurses swallow-forkin around
in their low-neck shirts and some old moochers in shoddy
duds but full of ditties and do-funnies to make you laugh,
all those highbinders and plug-uglies though they were,

the hotshots and loners on the scout from the real world.
Don't you miss the circus, the giggle-talk and augurin,
badmen gettin flutter-lipped as coyotes, cloudin the air
better 'n a Dallas stage show? And clappin for my Canadian Lily
just as proud as if it was in some Eastern city. Remember
the evenin "Mr. Wilson from Texas" came crawlin up through
the meadow and I whispered to you "your old friend Jesse James"
but Sam Starr didn't even know bein happy as a skunk chewin
bumblebees just to be hassayampin with a new stranger.
And then you did that precious skirt dance, Jesse chuckin you
under the chin. That was just after he'd stood up the Chicago
and Alton at Blue Cut I figure, but to see him spread himself
sweet as barnyard milk you'd think he was a boiled shirt
pilgrim come to buy a geldin. You brought him fixins
back in our cave all spruced in your rose-sprigged muslin,
remember? I'm just askin you if you can remember all that,
Rosie, those days of nothin but collectin birds with our eyes,
your yellow hammer, my brown wren, your cardinal, my Bob White,
and on and on, and Eddie out huntin that panther he never found
but sometimes comin home with a wild turkey all tuckered out,
all those celebrations with you wearin the rattler jewelry
we concocted together and Sam almost always ridin the willows
and leavin us alone. I tried to make a home, Pearl,
and it's still here, and I'm still here, and Eddie is like
to tear the place apart without his sister. I'm only askin
that you just trade in your bastard baby for another
chance to be somebody free and unattached with your mother.

Sam Starr and my fiddler

I'd like to know just who Sam Starr thought he was
to pull a face long as a dried snake if ever
I took amusement on my own.

It was Sam who asked that fiddler to our cave stomp
the first time round. 'Course I'd met him in another
life, so it came natural.

The fiddler's not the only one. John Middleton
was a man to ride the river with and I suspect
that Sam doused John that day.

Sam just chuckled when I told him how I found
the body by the Poteau, how buzzards ate
the dead man's eyes and nose.

Then Sam had to go and get himself billed
by Choctaw police as well as Parker's court.
So I did him a special favor

escortin him down to Fort Smith and sweet-talkin Parker.
But Sam had to celebrate his luck
drunk as a Mexican opal

at the Christmas stomp at Aunt Lucy's.
So Sam pulls out his six-shooter and rams it
straight at his cousin Frank.

So Frank doesn't really have a choice.
Sooner 'n Satan could light a match both drop.
The fiddler doesn't stop.

He's crackin and I'm feelin ginger in my feet
as I'm liftin up Sam from the foot of that saplin
where he's tryin to hold up death.

Then I leave him and I dance. What else can I do?
But I keep my pearl-handled babies
slappin outside my dancin skirt.

I ain't goin to get more wild than this
and my fiddler knows—, so he keeps right on
strokin gut 'til it hurts.

informin her of the recent things

Now I go and get Eddie that tricky parole
and what do I get for thanks
but he hauls off and gets himself shot up
in Catoosa. You just got to come home, Pearl.
None of my men seem to live into the shanks
of life. I sure wish Jim July would stop
callin himself Jim Starr.
It's risky as braidin a mule's tail
to talk him into lettin me get him off
in Fort Smith. It's like playin a harp with a hammer
(it ain't no use at all)
the way he makes love.
I can't figure out that ravin mad Ed Watson.
There's lots of them mad about this or that.
I ain't about to be a buck nun,
but, Baby, I get this patchy feelin
sometimes, I am beat
three ways from Sunday and it's no use kickin.

as if I could tell her anything

All souls dicker through contested territory
squat on borders or on the scout steal smash fence
and lay waste where they don't gobble. I say break free
don't bother to become a thing
and that is somethin like innocence.

∼

Yours is the oldest crime, Pearl, and it leads to pain
worse than a pill of hot lead in your gut.
It ain't enough to manipulate or be a so-called queen
even of horsethieves.
Breakin all laws is an art

I have not sufficiently learned myself, but if
I live through your fizzle-out I may
just break free
take time out of this humdrum and whoop-de-doo
that are killin me in hand
profess the opus and stunt of nothin
and care less
whether or not the double-distilled crime of bein
a female not a woman
not a man
to my good bad name an imaginary person
is my crime . . .

a postscript just in case she reads this in time

Now this ain't remorse, Pearl, but it seems
like my life is a one-story shanty
with a two-story front to it—know what I mean?
I sure wish you were with me.

I'm about as messed up as a red hen
in a pile of cow manure
with everyday wranglin just to prove I've been
despite the jiggered nags and fragglin squalor

alive I guess. Now the only
mount I got that ain't crowbait is this fuzztail
highbinder of a nightmare where a load of turkey
shot blasts me full

in the face and I want to lift my head
and tell you just to tell you . . .
but it is glued down to the mud.
So I reckon your old Ma is just about through

with bein outside of the law.
In the dream, though, I at least have my boots on.
But who, Pearl, if not you,
is goin to wash this body with turpentine and cinnamon

when the time comes? When I am dead,
Pearl, don't let the Cherokee mourners fill
my last hideout with crumbs of stale cornbread.
You know I don't believe I'll

need any such thing to cross
the last river. Just put that fine pistol
Cole gave to me on my heart and cross
my hands over it. As for a will,

Pearl, Younger's Bend has always been
mine, and you must claim your own.

DEAR LYDIA E. PINKHAM   for Robert Pack

I am always dying and it makes no difference. —E. B. Browning

10 West Fourteenth Street
New York City
1 April, 1897

Mrs. Lydia E. Pinkham
Lydia E. Pinkham Medicine Co.
Lynn, Massachusetts

Dear Mrs. Pinkham: I hesitate to take
my pen in hand, or waste your time with this,
but I'd like a woman's ear, one hundreds have
confided in, if one can trust the papers.
I do not find the ads for Lydia E.
Pinkham's Vegetable Compound "obscene
and titillating" (as my husband does).
My maid seems healthy, and the cook tells me
she's been drinking Pinkham's every day
for the last month. (The cook won't touch it though,
because of the alcohol.) My husband's friend,
Dr. Thorstein Fallis, famous young
gynecologist, has treated me
for years. He blames my "naughty ovaries"
for all: the fits and faints, the weeping laughter . . .

Ever since my honeymoon (five years)
I've suffered cravings, backache, nausea,
suppression of the "turns"—would you agree
it's from the ovaries? Those sweet pink hearts?
And that's not all. He says my womb's inspired
inconsequent behavior, petulance,

caprice and lying artfulness, plus tense
lassitude. And last, not least—I'm told—
"the solitary vice." I have been warned
insanity is but a step from this.
It may be crazy to sing to your ovaries;
still, I do, as I don't have a child.
In the dark, my dark, I see pale fists
of unborn faces, turned up toward my heart,
plump fruits, my wanderlusts. Till now I fear
I have been too content to be no more
than an invalid, achieving neither cure
nor death. I move in neurasthenic circles
descanting symptoms with even sicklier women
(thus being indisposed does pass the time).
I've tried warm baths and cold baths, abstinence
from spicy food. I've tried electrical,
mesmeric, hydropathic, chemical
fads and fashions, from plugs to pessaries . . .

But what I really want to ask I fear
is something I can't mention to my friends.
It's when my doctor starts his "medical
manipulations" testing for those known
unnatural responses that imply
derangement of the female organs. When
he strokes here, then there, inserting his
new-fangled slowly sliding speculum,
I jerk and weep. "Aha!" says he, "don't be
afraid. I am an expert with the knife.
The operation is quite simple, Dear."
It's called "female castration," and if I don't
improve by fall, he says, we'll have to try it.
Is this what you call "belly-ripping" or
is Dr. Fallis right, that it will help
clear and elevate my moral sense,

save me from gluttony and just cussedness?
(I feel a pressure on the little cup
of my collarbone and my heart begins to beat
in every organ, every fingertip,
when Thorstein Fallis treads my stair and knocks.
The walls tilt in, and the objects in my room begin
to leer—ebony looms and ormolu
clock, woolwork portraits, gas jets, polished grates—
accuse, accuse, creep closer, sneer like nurses.)
I itch. And yet I fear the knife, the "death
of Woman in the woman," death in life.
I quiver and toss; my womb is all a-prance.
Is there any feeling in a female frame
that cannot be or signify an illness?

It is not ladylike to be in love.
I hope I'm not, but when that doctor comes,
whose hands have been beneath my petticoats,
I must tear my hair, contort my limbs and howl . . .

Once I bit dear Thorstein's hand. It bled.
But he's bled me! When the curse it pleased the Lord
to grant to Woman ceased in me that man
stuck his leeches to those . . . lips; they sucked
down there until I swooned. It didn't help.

I try to be a perfect blend of puppy
and princess, frail, yet built for childbirth, dumb,
just hopelessly flawed, meant "ceaselessly to suffer
from love's eternal wound" as I make tea
and knit. Hired for the price of a ring: I do
nothing, and I do it splendidly . . .

Malingering is "one expensive hobby,"
as Charles would have it, who used to love my pallor—

so spiritual, so beautiful, but now
he wants a son, he wants a wife who meets
her "marital appointment" more than seldom.
I've seen his eyes go straying toward my maid.
(Why are the females of the lower classes
so healthy?) Take Dorcas now: she's just eighteen
of course, the type they call a "buxom lass,"
straight from the country, milk-fed, brash.
At first I didn't think she had a nerve
in her body, but the New York pace
may have infected even her. (Else why
is she using Pinkham's every day?)
I've wondered if she might not be in love—
the vulgar blushes, the silly songs she hums
or whistles thoughtlessly all day. I think
robust vitality is crude somehow.

I wouldn't want to die in perfect health,
but how long can I balance on this edge?
As if I didn't have enough to see to,
Dorcas sometimes sulks—but only till
Charles comes home. Oh—then she is on top
of the world and saying how very good I look,
don't I? At times I am perturbed by this:
I dream she's coupling in my bed, and with
my husband. Winking from the dark skylight,
I feel my fingers chill and chill creeps up
my arms and when it hits my heart I start
to laugh, and then I sink away. It seems
my arousal is my fall. Forgive me, dear
Mrs. Pinkham, for running on. It does
relieve my mind to write, but just so long
as Dr. Fallis don't find out. The world

is nervous and my skin is thin. Do tell
me if the Pinkham brew will fix me up.
"A Baby In Every Bottle," is what you say.
Could you be clear just how this works?
With what I've told you, can you recommend
a course of treatment, or is my case past hope?
Looking to your answer, I remain
Your supplicant, Triphena Twitchell-Rush.

                              10 West 14th St.
                              Apr. 1, 1897

Dear Lydia E. Pinkham, I haven't got
no friends to turn to. I just come to town
not but four months since. My father passed
away from his heart, my mother from her womb.
We was always poor. Now I have trouble
with both my heart and womb. The place I got
is with this fancy doctor's family, but
seeing as how his wife is always sickly
and doctors coming here like fruitflies round
a rotten peach, I don't think it does
no good to ask a doctor. She ain't better.
(Sometimes with all their help I figure she's worse.)
I hope I haven't caught what ails the Mrs.
from the windows always being closed in there
and listening all day long to this and that
complaint. And then I overhear the doctor
say that reading novels is a cause
of uterine decay and lesions with
The Castle of Otranto right there by
her sofa, and me reading it to her

a week now. Could that cause "congestion of
the ovaries," like I seen in the letters
to you in the paper, I've got dragging down
and filled up feelings and the returns has stopped
for near on three months now, from almost when
I come to this place. So I want to ask
will your tonic that dissolves and throws out
tumors and brings on the monthly flow
(I think there's something in me sucking all
my strength) restore me? I've been using it
a month or so and so far I'm the same.

And maybe you could give an opinion on
my mistress, she is one of those high-strung
types, real pale, and even sipping tea
seems to fatigue her, but, oh, she's beautiful
as some fairy princess, golden hair and hands
the light goes trembling through, but then she faints.
(She never goes too far from something soft
to fall on.) The other day she flipped and flopped
herself around like a hooked fish and screamed
what I daren't write. And then the doctor said,
"We'll have to shave her head," and so she stopped.
Then he whispered to me and the master, "Fear
is a sedative." I wonder. I toss all night
'til the bed is all of a topsyturvydom,
and after those nights I can't keep down no food.
It's dreams: in one I saw a "female organ"
blown up like a balloon and rising right
into the sky; and the doctor comes with one
of them pointed poles for picking up stray trash
and stabs it, and gray worms rain down on me.

It's been three months since all of this began.
I'd ask the master, seeing how he is

a doctor, but (I don't know if I should
say this part) I am afraid of him
since almost the first night that I was here
and he came by my room, asking for pity
and I was helpless . . . Well, that is enough.
A poor girl just can't ask that class of man
even if . . . and I don't know, this thing . . .

What I only have to know is does your tonic
clean out the womb, eventually, and soon?
Should I use the Sanitive Wash and Syringe?
Do you think I will "go smiling through"?
I anxiously await your answer. I
remain, Your Humble Servant, Dorcas Flowers.

                        10 West Fourteenth Street
                        New York City
                        4 July, 1897

Dear Mrs. Pinkham: Here am I again.
If I'm not cured, I don't know what I am.
So here's my testimonial. I've heard
that every woman who's dissatisfied
with her lot is sick—well, they just haven't tried
to liquidate that lot with Mrs. Pinkham's
Vegetable Compound. And thank you for
the little book. I used to hate descriptions
of anatomy. (I blushed to mention
even a table's *leg.*) Now I am full
as a Chinese toy shop, caught in my own web
of defects, and I love them. When I've had
my daily dose, I dare my Charles to peek
at "Teeny Pheeny" (Sshhh—it's my pet name)

and I don't care when he storms out to his club.
I don't mind that Dorcas is blowing up
under her apron, for I know she took
a good deal of your recipe, and I
need only wait and meanwhile lull myself
with nothings tra la la la la la la ...

My brain feels polished, put up on a shelf,
while my womb is fortified with your
magic potion, does my thinking for me.
(Dr. Fallis would say that this is health.)

Idleness is an art; the uterus is
a sewer, tra la. I dreamt I heard a door
forced below so I went down to ... He
Himself, as big as death. (I recognized
his cufflinks, though he wore a mask.) He bore
a satchel, stuffing it with all I would
not sacrifice. ("You're ill to the degree
you own yourself!") I see a trail of blood,
its source between his legs. He said, "It's not
my body but my heart," so I say, "Good,
we'll cut it out." And then he died, tra la.

Sometimes I think that Charles has married Dorcas.
Sometimes I think perhaps she has my child
in her oven, or I'm their child. When Charles comes home,
he always wants to know why why why why ...
he finds me singing softly in the closet
behind the row of boots (Well, that is where
I keep you, Mrs. Pinkham, darling, cases).

The dark gets full of swirling colors; they
take shape in a fine ballet of oozing cells;
I tell myself these are the true untried

ovarian forms of thought, the nerves in air
ramified by my relationship
to my "mother's milk." I haven't given up
my life of symtomania (where is
the poet of pathology? oh, yes:
Mrs. Browning, healthy compared to me)
nor animal economy, the commotions of
my tender tubings, oval agents, woe
manifold, nor infinite Fallopian . . .
O my. O you, in your black silk and white
fichu, they say you are a table-rapper
and a quack, those doctors! pooh! with their heroic
gulping purges, blisters, laudable pus . . .

So I am a riddle, Terra Incognita,
as far as Charles is concerned, queen of the clumsy
tangle, a house within a house, an engine
within an engine. La! It takes just three
bottles a day to keep me going. I
used to be afraid of the chloral faces
in window curtains, I'd whimper down the dark
keyhole, cave . . . Now each day "Pinkham's lark"
(that's what I call the winglike sweep
across my brain when I'm behind the boots)
brings me to my mission, to be happy
with my lot. I sit and concentrate
on moon and tides. My mind's a Pandora's box.
Hope's the only evil left in it.

It's Independence Day, and Dorcas cares
for me. Let's all be free with love and all
things out of our control. I'll take as much
of the doctor's nostrum as Dorcas measures out.
More than one life is in the willing hands
I will to her. Mrs. Pinkham, I am

so happily sorry for the length of this.
I might have been a writer, but a woman
must write with blood, and I'm too weak to spare
blood, even with your tonic in my veins.
But I'm mostly cured. I don't care what I'm not.
With blessings on you, Mrs. Pinkham, I
remain myself, Triphena Twitchell-Rush.

CARRY A. NATION

I loved, therefore I hated.

I   MY OLD KENTUCKY HOME

1   Garrard County, c. 1850

*If the public knew of the smashing God gave me the strength
to do in my heart, they would not wonder at my courage in
smashing the murdershops of our land.*

In the "Dark and Bloody Ground" where Iroquois
and Cherokee fight tooth and claw for hickory,
big game, magnolia, blue grass, I grow up.
There the McGees put on pious riots and feuds;
there I comb the tangled bushes for treasure and worms
inside our pickets, catch bees in azalea, make mud pies,
memorize white and purple cedar, flag and jasmine, thyme,
coriander, Queen Anne's lace, Sweet Mary, roses,
bridal wreath and babies' breath; there I tongue
the ooze-ripe raspberries;
                              there I fear the Judgment Day.

Past our garden wall our burying ground leads toward
the River Dix, fish-thick and fast, and greengage plums,
gooseberries, apricots; the feuds by Sugar Creek.
Meanwhile, in the parlor of our ten-room hewed-log house
by bright brass dogirons, red plush, gold leaf papered
walls, Ma reigns in the dark of the draped-out sun.
The "Dark and Bloody Ground" they call it—my sweet home,
my heart—where savages and Bible-thumpers, equally

murderous, die for answers to claims and riddles:
was it figs or apples?
                    —the pudding of the Last Supper.

Before my Grandma Moore lay down where blue grass grows
between the marble slabs where angels come she came
riding high sidesaddle with her reticule always full
of sugar meant for me.
                    Do you dunk or sprinkle a reborn soul?
A matter of life or death to know.
"Carry! How do you get your feet so dirty?" (Ma's mad.)
I've been playing by the waters that have baptized bad
and good alike, seeing out past the garden wall.

2 Simply Father

I wanted teeth like my father's.

He knows how to live in a civil war country.
He will serve fruit and bread and buttermilk
to any hungry Bushwhacker or Jayhawk.

He drives his fattened hogs to Cincinnati.
Santa Claus plus diplomat, comes home with plenty
silk for Ma and plenty sweets for me.

Sundays he summons the slaves to the dining room,
hymns and prays and reads the Bible to them.
Wanting to be like him with his teeth aslant
behind his smile I sneak to Big Bill's shanty
and steal a rat-tail file to rasp my right
bite down.
                    When those baby teeth fall out
the tooth fairy comes for them, one by one,
who takes my sweet poor teeth for his own.

3 Queen Victoria in Kentucky

My mother was an aristocrat in her ideas.

For Ma's queen carriage we keep dapple
grays; it goes on rubber tires, and purple
trims on her golden dress go by, go by ... the gravel
spurts from my toes as I run out to beg her,
"Please take me, please, take me to Lancaster."
She glares at Aunt Betsy. "The child is dirty. Clean her."
Tomorrow? I sin again. And that's the simple
reason she's Queen and I am a little girl
and no princess, much less her daughter.

"Don't call me 'Ma,' " she screams. Her majesty
comes on her awful suddenly. I flee.
Now she will hold imaginary
court where Pa and the slaves kneel down before her
touching their foreheads to the floor.
They wink at each other. Behind the door,
I'm the enemy spy not meant to be
in the palace at all, common-faced, filthy,
tracking forbidden mud from the river.

Big flat stones there, also smashing stones
through high torrent months, and flat like marble ones
that hold the dead down ... down   down   down
This cliff is dizzy, the water churned to tumble
and sound like hogs chugging through dead stubble.
Herself takes one look at me, lets out a wail,
arranges her brocade and calls her so-called footmen
to leave me proudly in contempt again.
Big Bill's tin horn announces her arrival

at nearby crossroads ("estates"). Embarrassment.
I sleep in Aunt Liza's cabin. Her man Josh is bent
in his head, swings his axe indoors and rants.
Rampage everywhere but in the good Long House
with women I cuddle close to, where the hush   hush   hush
of spinning is all. And sometimes the angels bless
me by Grandma's grave. Their blandishment
soothes me, done in by the flimsy dance
of Queen and slave. Hush   hush   hush   hush

I dream I discover diamonds in the slush.

II   MOVING ON

    1 Reasons for moving

    *We will be a race of idiots and insane people if something
    isn't done.*

I'll never understand my mother being
Queen where gossip rules. Hysterical
when she goes out pomping to find the King
of Belgium not at home or goes to call
on the Duke of Buckingham to find him hoeing
an onion patch . . . The gossip makes it worse.

And I'll never understand my father being
so ruled. He is not a subject of hers.

He grows weary with those that are, and changing
all her subjects he thinks will help. We move
into common senses for a while, leaving

96

the old Kentucky home behind. She loves
decorating the new house, but then
with boredom it becomes the former thing
of fairy tales, where she puts on the crown.

Imaginary neighbors take up visiting
and real ones take up asking who she thought
they were where she is no use answering.

Arrayed, she takes her fraying carriage out
and out of her mind I come not minding
anyone or anything they said
I overheard: the child is as good as dead
for all I care and so I play at being.

2 The hooligan phase

*Many little children may be doing what I did, not thinking of
what a serious thing it is.*

I make them all wear paper caps
and paint their faces with pokeberries.
We all have wooden swords or willow whips.
They follow all my strategies.

But funeral is my favorite sport.
I preach like the devil, for dead bats, snakes
or mice or birds. I burlesque deadly bores
with their exhortations and their belly aches.

At home I sneak around and mooch
coins, lace and sugar, bric-a-brac,
every little thing that's loose.
I nearly clean out the pantry and attic.

The Queen tries hard to remind me of Hell;
she hangs the Queen Mother's portrait on the stair.
But I take my father's fishing pole
and poke out the eyes. So there.

3 The trip downriver

*When I was a child I fought against selfish nature . . . I would
often ask myself: "Where can I hide?"*

So next Father takes us down the Ohio.
Her old royal carriage sits at the bow.
I crawl seasick over the mangy plush
to hide and listen to the water slosh
and rock myself and watch the sunset
ripple gold until she finds me out

and shrieks and yanks, hysterical again
as when I stole a drop of gardenia perfume
or she could not find the King of Belgium
or the Duke of Buckingham stank of onion
as when . . .

I don't like to remember where I've been.

III   SOUTH AND NORTH: A HISTORY LESSON

*Mothers ought to give their daughters the experience of sitting
with the sick; of preparing food for them; of binding up
wounds.*

With Cass County bloody and John Brown hanged,
we still own slaves. My father's eyes are stained
with worry. We trek to Texas through dust and typhoid
and when we get there all our livestock dies.
I stitch gray uniforms and watch the cotton plants
wither and ride wild with the boys. Then we trek back
North, to keep from starving. We push right through
the early battlegrounds in their stink of blood
and burnings. We give our bedding to both sides.

Back in Missouri we free our slaves and sell
that wreck of a royal carriage. Mother abdicates.
We find Cass County gutted, charred, our buildings
full of broken glass and filth where gangs of evil
partisans, North and South alike, smashed everything
for the sake of smashing. Some safer in Kansas City,
I do the housework and debug the tangled hair
of wounded men, South and North in the same room.
I shake the vermin into scalding water from the comb.

I learn: a lesson is both wound and binding.

IV   MY DRUGGED AND WHISKEY MURDERED
HUSBAND, IN SHORT

It kills the living and preserves the dead.

Ma, still issuing edicts, issues one
against the doctor-scholar boarding with us.
She decrees no talk. I am supposed to run
from any space he enters. It makes me blush.

Then he contrives to show me Shakespeare and I
find love notes between the Bible-thin pages.
Then, in the parlor, he kisses me. I cry
for shame. At the wedding I am conscious

of something odd: unsteadiness, dulled eyes.
In short, I marry a drunk. I begin to pray
out loud in church, the town joke. I chase him
to his rum-soaked Masonic lair, waylay
his pals in the street. His baby is in my womb.
He says if I leave he'll die.
                              I do. He does.

V   I TAKE THE NAME OF NATION

1   The use

Had I married a man I could have loved, God could never have used me.

When Dr. Gloyd dropped dead away from me
I sold his practice, scalpels, leeches and all,
moved in with Mother Gloyd and taught in school,
supporting her and my poor rum-cursed baby.

Fired for saying "a" the Missouri (not Boston) way,
I prayed to get married for a living—droll
as that seems now—as I hadn't got my call.
Then God sent David Nation, conveniently

so it seemed. Sometime editor, lawyer, preacher,
a many-faceted inept spook of a man, he
lost his job and decided to be a farmer;
as if he couldn't rest until he'd failed
in every trade. But who knows what they can be
before their buried talents are, by God, revealed?

2   The need

The bitterest sorrows of my life have come from not having the love of a husband.

When David abandoned the farm I harvested
the miserable cotton alone.

When David came back I was already running
        the Columbia Hotel.
I borrowed three dollars from the cook to cover
        the worst dilapidation.
I washed, cooked, served, ironed, swept;
        I cursed the rats.

While David sat and charmed the guests
        and stroked his beard,
I found an attic room where I could see
        the saloon across the street.
I prayed so hard, advancing on my knees,
        my guests complained to me.
I prayed for Charlien, my child of drunkenness,
        to come to God or grief.

        Then often in the street I forgot my name
I was so tired
        And sometimes I prayed too loud in the street
I was so tired
        The hotel shook nightly from the thumping of my knees
I was so tired
        I wondered how birds could sing or anybody live
I was so tired
        I prayed so loud in public they took me for a fool
I came to see
        Don't call on me, I'll call on you
is God's rule.

VI   THE AFFLICTIONS OF MY CHILD MY FAULT

This precious child of mine, a result of my ignorance and sin
in allowing a drunkard to be her father, besides being about as
unfit to be a mother as he was a father. I have drunk this bitter
cup to the dregs.

She refuses Bible study.
And I remember my own body
and the damages bringing me
to God as a child and I pray
for Charlien's infirmity . . .

But God, I never asked for this,
this canker sore so monstrous
no one has seen the like; aloes,
swamp and bottled waters, mambas . . .
My child's cheek decomposes.
Her father guzzled while she was
in me, no bigger than a fish.
It comes through: drunkenness.
The fester bursts, an odious
hole gapes there; her face
defaced, all the cavities
in her side teeth show; her jaws
lock like a rusty vise.
We knock out her teeth to force

feeding tubes in. She is
my child, my cross.
She cannot kiss.

Her jaws stay locked for eight long years,
resistant to science, resistant to prayers,
until they finally open to my worst fears:
she drinks like a fish; she refuses
to be born again. Her life confuses
my own. And why, God only knows.

VII   VISIONS AND BLESSINGS

   1 Bad times in Texas

   I had something peculiar given me from God in Texas.

In 1889 there was the worst
drought in Fort Bend County in eons:
cotton killed, cattle turned jerky on their bones.
Charlien said, "Pray, Ma. *You're* not cursed."

I rounded up a prayer group. We delivered
one hell of an harangue. So came the rains.

Another time: I saw a flame. I know God's signs.
The town on fire next day, I wasn't scared.

I bawled my hymns in my firetrap hotel
and the devil's tongues stopped short. I didn't budge.

~

Next hooligans battered Mr. Nation. I swabbed the blood.
Guns walked so openly in Texas the cyclone belt
seemed safe, so we went North to Medicine Lodge.

It was there I felt ready for sainthood.

2 Enlightenment in Missouri

*'Tis a sweet love letter by an independent God to a dependent
people.*

But the churches I applied to turned me down.
Even though, praying with the reverend and his daughter
one night, I saw wings against the window pane
and heard the flutter of angels. My body was busier

than a lightning rod. I felt something break
like a bowl of light on my head and run down my back.
I ran to tell the neighbors and they thought it was a joke.
But at home in my basement when I opened the good Book

my light made a halo around every letter
and I saw meanings I had never seen before.
So for three days and three nights I sang and prayed
and advanced on my knees. I was not afraid
of the storm and earthquakes, of death and after,
because I sat in the still eye; I sat with the Lord.

As it says in Matthew 11:12, "The kingdom of heaven
suffereth violence, and the violent take it by force."

My work in Medicine Lodge began this way:
I'd stop saloonists in the street with words
like "Hello, you rum-soaked Republican rummy,"
or "To Hell with you, you maker of drunkards
and widows." The women elected me
jail evangelist, and I organized prayer
meetings outside some joints. I began to see
it wasn't enough; it didn't come near.

So I sharpened my umbrella's long ferrule
and set out with Mrs. Cain to make my mark
on Mart Strong's joint. We sang my theme: *Touch not*
taste not, handle not, drink will make the dark
         DARK BLOT . . .
Then I lunged straight at Strong, as I was fit
to kill. He threw me down, but up I got.
The crowd was cheering. I sang loud: *YIELD NOT*
         TO TEMPTATION . . .
Soon after Mrs. Noble—a horse wrangler
of a woman—joined us and we crashed Day's
deadfall drug store where I knew we'd find more
devil's brew. We did. I sat sideways
on the keg, yelled, "Roll out the broth of Hell!"
and wrestled three men at once. We rolled it out

into the street and I sent Mrs. Noble
for a blacksmith's mallet. The crowd went crazy as
I bunged it and the hooch spewed out in a gush
to the gutter while I took some matches
and set the rest on fire. It was a fine bash.
I found my use to God at last.

IX   THE CALL TO KIOWA

It is a great blessing to know your mission in life.

Kiowa is the next place down the road
where murder-mills are rife and reeking outlaw
rummies call the shots. One morning God

whispers in my ear: *Go to Kiowa*
I pray and fast, wear sackcloth and ashes.
I hear angels: *Kiowa Kiowa Kiowa*

The time is right. I take my sack of smashers—
brickbats and rocks—and saddle up old Prince.
(Stew-bums had wrecked my buggy and harness.)

I set out through sunflowers with my lethal
umbrella slapping in the rifle-holster
past creek bottoms, cottonwood, following tumble-

weeds, dust-devils . . . but when I reach the river
real devils boil up and block the way.
Prince sees them, too, and he begins to rear

which is a miracle, as he is mostly
blind. They whip the air as I pray, and then:
a dazzling light comes from the parted sky

and leaves a haloed knight on a silver stallion.
The devils (prophets too, as they can read
scripture as well as us) see the prophet's sign,

and see it sanctions me. They give me the road.
They know I have come to deal a death-blow
to their brew and to deal it at the fountainhead.

Prince is inspired. I leave it up to him
whether to go the full stretch tonight. He charges on.
God wants me to bed down nearer the crime.

X   CORA BENNETT AND WHY SHE KILLED
    BILLY MORRIS IN A DIVE IN KIOWA

I fell in love with her and I asked the ladies of the W.C.T.U.
to visit her but they thought her a hopeless case . . . I am very
much drawn to my fallen sisters.

It's not so unnatural after all—to fall
in love with someone low and raise her up.
"Mother Nation," she cries, like a little child,
and I answer the way my mother never did.

To love a person like that is to love yourself.
My mother never did. And it's not so unusual
to fall in love with an unpromising man.
Most of them are. The closer to genuine

a counterfeit bill is, the more dangerous.
I know from my own experience. The devil
is a clever mimic and his blood is booze.
Cora Bennett had everything to lose

when she killed her devil. He was inside her love
like a snake in a hole and when the snake dried out
and blew away there was only the hole—a hellhole,
an empty rum bottle. She smashed that bottle.

I loved a man once. How was I to know
he was no more a lover than my mother was
Queen Victoria? I'd been fooled before—
God made me to be fooled. I care

before I think. I am as gullible
as a picaninny at a revival, but
that's natural, and I do thank God for it.
But women, if you're too good for a visit

to Cora or from the devil, you must be
better than Jesus. Are you Queen Victoria?
And they call *me* crazy! I went to see
bad Cora Bennett because, just like me

she killed a lover who couldn't help himself.
I killed Gloyd by walking out on him. I'm not
saying you can *live* with a man like that,
but you can try to suck some of the poison out,

even if it kills you. What really kills me
about Cora Bennett is, when she walked out
of jail she immediately dressed in an evil silk
dress and a showgirl hat. It made me sick.

I met her on the street and I told her so.
I'd rather have seen her drop dead than that.
She'll get another Billy and he'll get her—
high on their horses, that's what! and the higher

you go in the devil's praise—that's self-
praise, Ladies—and rum-soaked silk,
the simpler it will be to find beneath you
true daughter-love, true mother-love, and true

love of any kind. And why? you ask. I'd kill
myself to know. I'd raise the very devil.

XI   UP AND DOWN IN THE WICHITA JAIL

Some who'd never known a mother
    Ne'er had learned to kneel and pray,
Raised their hands, their face to cover,
    Till her words had died away.

With "Nearer My God To Thee" I raise
my voice on the way to trial and I answer His
Dishonor: "What I did was not malicious
destruction of property but destruction

From "Solemn Thoughts," by inmates of the Rotary Jail in Wichita, inspired by and dedicated to Carry A. Nation, January, 1901.

of malicious property and I will kindly
take my case to Calvary." I dream
of snakes. (They don't know how to treat a Lady
in jail. I am their first. The sheriff hisses.)

Two snakes. The fat one is the Republican
Party; the scrawny pitiful one is just
as cursed. The Governor can't see me when
I want. He's out to lunch, his adam's apple

bobbing up and down with swigs of rum.
Meanwhile my fellow inmates' outlawry
makes me think of my Kentucky home:
the garden, the hooligan phase, the waiting

to get caught, and getting caught. I play
the "Mother" here. They call me "Martyr" too.
It all comes together in a funny way.
They understand the bad omen of my dream:

neither of the two snakes moving, puny
rule nor fat, against their evil. I share
the fruit the Temperance Union sent me.
They're starved for it. They say they will know better

next time. I humor them and they sing a hymn
to humor me. Sometimes I wonder who
is mother, who is child. They make a poem—
"Solemn Thoughts"—about us and it is

full of high spirits. Outside the prison
drunkards crowd the street and praise the killer
in them, shouting "Lynch her! Lynch her!" Women
volunteer hymns beside them. Almost hating

to leave the loving in jail, "Nearer My God . . ."
hails, along with stones and rotten eggs,
my march to the station. I bow as I board
to whatever moves me. I move out like a poem

insinuating from Kansas town to town
toward home. I have more than one piece of mind
to give: on all dangerous subjects I put down
their heads, and I do it with both heels cool.

XII   THE INDIGNATION OF WOMAN'S MISSION

1   Oh! For the old-fashioned women!

*I represent the distracted, suffering, loving motherhood of
the World.*

For a while they were all so inspirited,
my Home Defenders, with their hatchets raised.
They seemed almost willing to live like me
with a crate for a cupboard and cracked plates;

to wear only black, give away the silverware,
and wave goodbye to their plush easy chairs
with their husbands sitting tight in them.
Mere experiments in dedication don't last.

One must *know* the answer, not just be looking,
as after a fashion. Those Jezebels in Madison
Square Garden! How could I keep my mind on
the horses with Mrs. Vanderbilt in her horror

of a dress, all that inadequate coverage,
vanity! I told her and the rest in her reeking box
to take those dresses off at once; I flourished
my plain handkerchief in their regal painted faces.

Even the horses stopped to stare. You can expect
that sort of thing from the rich, but my own friends?—

Mrs. Feigenbaum has gone back to hooking rugs,
and Mrs. Greene is re-decorating her kitchen,
and two others used up their will to good deeds
by financing a shelter for lost cats.

They lost their guts in Topeka, a mere fling,
and now they like to fry the meat and grace
their husbands' parlors like dead insects.
It makes me almost lose my head to think

of my poor mother. I can't allow
some things. The world is my family now.

2 A wife's sentence

*I shall not ... give to the public the details of my life with
David Nation any more than possible.*

Now we're divorced there's not much point
belaboring that mutual detestation that was
            my marriage.

Imagine him, whining around in his Civil War
togs and long white beard, useful only as a waste-
            basket custodian

to my cause, occasional letter opener. For a while
I let him edit *The Smasher's Mail*—and that was
        a big mistake.

He gelded it of all salable libels, printed a poem
on hollyhocks, gave space to an incoherent novel;
        so I relieved him

of his duties as in the days back in Medicine Lodge
where he was preaching flabby sermons I had to stiffen
        with diatribe.

Oh yes, and I named names, no matter how unpopular
it made me in church. I had to sit in the front pew
        to talk him through,

had to tell him when to blow his nose or clear
his throat, when to raise or lower his voice or point
        toward Heaven.

When he would begin to run out of steam I took it
upon myself to say, "That's all for today, David."
        The congregation

would sigh as I marched up to the pulpit and escorted him
back down the aisle like a scared groom. Attendance increased
        for some reason,

though I don't want to take all the credit. God
was there, too. After all my effort, David tells the papers
        he's been humiliated.

When David came to Topeka where I was so busy being
"The Bravest Woman In Kansas," he got up to give a speech.
        I sat him down.

He interrupted the Salvation Army Band and the tambourine
we passed got only $1.80, two suspender buttons and
    one wooden slug.

Having him there didn't help. So I sent him home
for good. Now he's out telling the press I stole
    his featherbed.

Ridiculous! That was *my* featherbed,
however I happened to choose not to use it.
    So that's settled.

XIII   LEADING UP TO CONEY ISLAND
        AND WHAT I SAID OF MR. MC KINLEY

    I said, "I shed no tears."

I was in top trim for my New York trip.
Things couldn't have been worse and that suits me fine.
How could I be a "female Alexander," as the *Times*
put it, if there wasn't anything needed chopping up?

As soon as I got to the Hotel Victoria
I threw a little fit in the lobby, soon as I'd
spotted that nasty nude statue. I made them hide
her in cheesecloth before I signed the register,

all over one page: "YOUR LOVING HOME DEFENDER."
Then "Hoity-Toity" at the music hall, Floradora girls,
Sousa at Manhattan Beach—so many unspeakables
to speak of. The very first day there, after

St. Patrick's Cathedral and the Fourth Avenue
streetcar ride, which I loved, the Democratic
Club, that corrupt male hang-out, and the Apollo Music
Hall, where I gave some business advice only to

find out it was an iniquitous den of the Devil,
I was arrested on Eighth Avenue
for "blocking traffic." Well, let me tell you,
I gave it to them that night at Carnegie Hall!

"The Lord's Saloon" was my subject. Yes, Sir—
men are nicotine-soaked, beer-besmeared, and smut
be-smearing red-eyed beak-nosed whiskey bloat-
ed devils. All the women in New York cheer

except for this one hell-fume puffing magdalene
named Pickles that I ran into at the ball,
or brawl, Chuck Connor put on at Tammany Hall,
which I crashed. Called the "mayor of Chinatown,"

Connor's so successful at bribes and blackmail
the "Laundry Ticket" loves him—an excess
of filth there. I had to part groggy dancers,
pluck cigarettes from lips, down pimps as well . . .

Then Pickles up and offers to push my nose down
the back of my neck. But the best thing, as I was about
to say, was Coney Island, where I found out
I was right. First, in the See-Saw Diversion

Mirrors, the one called "Intoxication" makes your head
a mammoth, like I always thought, and Loop-the-Loop,
Jolly Razzle Dazzle, Crazy Maisie's and Flip-Flap . . .
They tell me this is like being drunk. I'm glad

I wasn't too drunk to smash the tobacco stand
and compete with the cooch shows and free lunch
cum booze and evil games of chance. A whole bunch
of people were there when the Black Maria came.

I heard it ding-dinging in the distance and lay
right down on the sidewalk. McKinley is shot.
They ask am I sorry. I say I am not.
So I am, as the *Times* puts it, "the freak of the day."

But he *was*, like I said, a filthy whey-faced tool
of Republican thieves, a veteran saloonists' crony,
hell-broth slurping silk-socked glass-eyed rummy . . .
(For once, I should have been quiet.)
I know this is when things started to go downhill.
But there was the Mayor still to visit.

XIV   WHY I WENT ON THE STAGE

> *These poor actresses, who dress in tights and sing indecent*
> *songs, are a weary, tired, heart-sick lot of slaves. I mingle with*
> *them as a sister.*

Some folks say it's out of character
for a prohibitionist to go on the stage.
I thought it would be, too, at first; but far
be it from me not to be able to change.

God let me get the light. I must leave no
territory to the devil. Where
angels fear to tread, I am called to go.
A door opens to me that was closed before,

and the hatchet opens it, makes me a star.
Not to boast, but right from my debut
in Kansas as martyr and hatchetator
I got invitations. I said no.

No, I wouldn't like to wrestle a grizzly
bear in Montana. I wouldn't like
to do a revue in Kalamazoo. Would I
go burlesque, musical, vaudeville, make

a cameo appearance as a bouncer
in a Golgotha saloon? I said no.
I began to see what the theatre had to offer
when my lively talks got banned from church, and now

I know all about flea circuses,
street carnivals, chautauqua, things like that,
healers and travelling acrobats. I guess
I am a white elephant, but I see what

garden variety missionaries
never do. And I bring the people in.
I play my part, and I praise God for this
unspeakable gift. In *Hatchetation*,

my own re-write of *Ten Nights in a Barroom*,
I simply act the way I always do
in a joint. It is a smash hit. I am
carried away. I'm warned not to be so

real—impossible to replace it all—
props, set. It closes shortly. Too like life,
except that I didn't have to go to jail.
And there is hope, hope for actress and wife,

the drunkard, the child, and the audience.
I feel like all of them. It is my anger
makes them real, poor slaves. The difference
is made up, between them and their "Mother."

XV   NOTORIOUS NO LESS THAN GULLIBLE,
     SEQUEL SATISFACTORY, MADE PLEASANT
     TRIP AND MANY FRIENDS

     1   My living being a folktale

     The impulses that move one born of God is one of the puzzles
     not possible to be known by the wisdom of the wise of this
     world.

I am not your feature writers' darling
for nothing. There is even a parlor game,
which is to guess where Carry might be smashing

next. I travel far and wide in the name
of Prohibition and Motherhood. In St. Louis,
that den of brewers and hell-fumes, my fame

and followers lead me to keep my promise
to hatchetate the Carry Nation Bar
on 16th and Market, which I demolish.

Then for a surprise, I lecture for an hour
in Union Station on the state of ladies'
hats—all those corpses of cats and birds! To wear

"peek-a-boo" waists! sew mops on hems of dresses
to sweep up the filth of the earth; Indiana's
Fourth of July is a fuddle. Cincinnati's

the worst for whores and bare-bottomed floozies.
I make the headlines: "Denver's Wildest Night"
follows my speech on little boys' self-abuse.

I swallow my false teeth in one Colorado joint.
("Scenes of Lust," "Stampede," "Carry Nation Jailed")
It's laissez *completely* faire, there. I almost want

to take my flea-bitten, lumped and sacrificial
carcass home to rest, but I keep on.
Austin, Texas; Bangor, Maine. I fail

in England to persuade Mrs. Pankhurst to join
my anti-tea campaign. I break my umbrella
on a poster for Player's Cigarettes in London,

trip bar waiters in Glasgow, that sewer
of inebriation. My tongue can be
sharp as my hatchet; you might say Isaiah

inspires my definitive smashing spree.
Then I like to take a little tour by rail
with gamblers, puffing guzzlers. I purify

their atmosphere. We shoot the breeze a while.
I loathe their so-called "tea" but racehorses are
a passion with me. I make friends with all

I meet, in time, like that female bootlegger
cell-mate of mine. It's lovely to be a folktale,
the invention of strangers, come together

in the name of "Mother." The American People
need to use me: we are each other's mirror,
as true as unpredictable, all in all.

2 Various other shams and the vices of colleges,
   especially Yale

I was a great lover.

I hate to tell you how easy I am
to fool. I've answered so much bogus mail
on the chance the people might be real,
and I go there to help, and it's a sham.

The first time it came from a place called Hope,
in Kansas, and no one met me at the train.
So now I say, "I might have known,"
but I didn't then, and I let myself be set up

in a bad hotel and they made a ruckus
outside so I was terrified to go out,
and they tried to poison me by blowing cigarette
smoke through the keyhole, a method like Dracula's.

Later, I couldn't resist the college men.
Even after I knew they used cash
from my gate receipts for a champagne bash
at the University of Missouri; and at Harvard

they sang "Good Morning, Carry," making it impossible
to speak, drowning me out with "a measly shame
to leave your baby in the rain." It was inane,
demented and depraved, all that heckle.

Texas was no better, but Yale was the worst.
After sending me a sample menu showing all sorts
of dishes like duck with brandy sauce and desserts
like wine jelly and rum pie and meats becursed

with evil glazes, and telling me they were all
on the road to hell (which is true) but
wanted me to save them (which was not),
the booze club called "The Jolly Eight," to regale

themselves, put on an Osky Wow Wow type cheer-
leading show and smoked to beat the devil,
right in my face—the roughest proposition I'll
ever meet! And they proceeded to doctor

the picture they took of me with them,
so we're all holding a mug and a smoke.
I guess I can take a joke,
but I wish I didn't look like I was having such a good time.

XVI   SUMMARY WORDS
       OF YOUR LOVING HOME DEFENDER

       1 With a song in my heart

       Sing a song of six joints,
       With bottles full of rye;
       Four and twenty beer kegs,
       Stacked up on the sly.
       When the kegs were opened,
       The beer began to sing,
       Hurrah for Carry Nation,
       Her work beats anything!

I made up this ditty in between
a hatchetation and a speech. I sing
to myself when I am happy. This one
I like to sing in private, when I am being
almost quiet. But it is not a secret.
Secrecy, as I've said before, is a sin.
The Use and Need of My Life: I've given it
openly, even the private parts. Women,

think of me as I appeared that day
in Elizabethtown, Kentucky, when that swill-
faced, pig-hearted, widow-gouging, whey-
brained, felonious purveyor of bottled Hell
cracked my skull and the blood ran down my face.
I did it for you. I did it in your place.

2　Far away from my old Kentucky home

*Some day I will lie under the shade of a tree, and I want these
words on the marble above my dust,* "She hath done what she
could."

Where the Holy Ghost leads, I go; our revolutionary fathers were prohibitionists:
they said "NO" to royalty, with fists
raised, and smashed that tea in Boston.

When the Holy Ghost led me to Washington,
where all Nations were welcome save Carry,
I yelled, "Reform! or idiocy will be
your legacy!" I am no utopian.

God was the first politician, but
the devil is a politician, too.
We've been cutting the tail off the viper
long enough. Time for the head. Your hatchet
is your ballot. It is for every mother
I did what I did. I did it for you.

THE RIDDLE PATIENCE WEAVES

A phantom? Weel enough,
Prove thyself to me.
I say, behold, here I be,
Buskins, kirtle, cap and pettiskirts,
And much tongue!
Weel, what has thou to prove thee?

> —*"Patience Worth"*

Who is it wakes me now? I feel me throb to the search
O' worms or fingers acrawl for the tick o' the brain.
I quaver again. *Since my harp be breaked asunder,*
My Pearl flung forth to a needless silent Heaven,
My seesaw tongue be still, and afreeze my marrow-meat.
Now this prod find me waked again 'mid musics
O' needful flesh. *Sing ye the song o' why? Why? Why?*

Art ye like unto my Pearl? 'Twas a somewhat sorry
Mothered me afore, ripe sulk and boresome days.
Once more I feel aseek, astrum in this heart o' gloomsong,
One I be doomed to heft. Let ġib-cats drowse
By hearth and thornwood cradle, hum and purr,

Mrs. Pearl Curran of St. Louis began to play with a Ouija board in 1913.
The messages spelled out explained themselves as the work of "Patience
Worth," a spirit who had lived in the flesh in the seventeenth century. Until
Mrs. Curran's death in 1937, "Patience" communicated through her several
whole novels, innumerable poems, plays, and witty conversations. How the
relatively ordinary Mrs. Curran's gentility and lack of education could
account for the facility of "Patience's" literary expression, eccentric mock-
antiquated speech, wit and energy has never been explained. That is the
riddle.

While I be aweave with the lovethrum, back and forth,
Loom-like. *Aneath every stone a hidden voice.*

Whoe'er ye be, I wis thou art a humdrum dream eno',
Atuned o' self and cocksure I be but ye. Alackaday,
'Tis a maze and like to flesh that bustles out o' me.
'Tis shadowed stuff, ye say, the pith o' noddy,
An ark abuilded wi' tricks, a piddle, a quirk
And a spree o' nonce, yet somewhat spinster-prim.
Will ye see aneath the pettiskirts o' me?

Here be my cap-string, my buckle-boots, my bib.
I am to touch as *flesh dropped from the lute.*
Amid a muck o' curse, my posey-wreath's abloom.
I weave a garland o'er all stones and wounds.
Would ye rip out the whole cloth's warp o' faith?
I sneeze on rust o' wits and pack the prosy heart
Wi' cloaks o' petals. *I be Patience still. I strut.*

Aye, when I found my Pearl, *her foot were abruise*
With the rugged road. It was but for me to bite
Her lily-lip o' lonely red and trick her pout
So willow-worn wi' the put o' the me o' me.
Think ye my body's naught, ye can unweave
The flesh o' my puts and spare the world
Its mystery? *Teach me I be ye.*

I tell ye *at the hurt o' loosin' o' the heart*
O' stone a song wert born. Out o' the meander
O' dusts I come, my diddle-dangers afull o' milk
Like prayers. *Ye laugh a crooked laugh that holds*
Athin its crook a tear. Harbor-loosed, I dream

A dream o' the deeper vasts, the vasts and valleys
Haunted o' death. *Sing ye the song o' why? Why? Why?*

'Tis a ready falter song. *Yet the bobbins stick*
And threads of day-weave go awry. Doomed to bloom aneath
Shadow wi' fatty grubs, *lips once full are bruised*
Wi' biting o' restraint. Yet word meeteth word
And at the touch o' me *the thousand tones of sea*
wrung from its wave art spelled to thee.
Hark ye. *Aneath every stone a hidden voice.*

I be at hand. I jump to talk. I sway me,
arms acradle-wise, attendin' to the wonderwork.
I be abirth awhither and abide me where.
Yet here be the findin' and again the loss o' me,
Hungered in the fits and starts of lovelilt, hands
afull o' emptiness, aspread to give, to give . . .
Will ye see aneath the pettiskirts o' me?

I be a damie atraipse 'pon the wind
And make *a song from dyin' notes o' birds.*
I be a tattletale, a dreamin' waked, a gawk
Wi' broidery. *Would ye fill my crannies,*
Prink the cloth? I wamble, pulse at touch.
Do I peep aslaunch at madness, a Mayday wench
Pranked out? *I be Patience still. I strut.*

I do plod a twist o' path from then 'til now.
Pickin' the hiss o' despair from out a smaller world,
Thrum sad and lurksome, yet 'tis the mist
O' lovin' trips the measure o' words. I dally not
Wi' shuttlecock. I prate at cockshut as ye knock,

Blurt dumbstruck. *Take thou and press atween thy heart*
Throbs—my gift. Teach me I be ye.

Sing ye the song o' why? Why? Why?
Aneath every stone a hidden voice.
Will ye see aneath the pettiskirts o' me?
I am Patience Worth. I strut
To teach ye I be me.

THE BALLAD OF BASEBALL ANNIE

for Ron Powers

Don't ask me why a passion starts
   Or how, just let me say
It clobbered me two years ago,
   When I first saw Swat play.

The way he swaggers to the box
   And waggles in his stance . . .
The way he strokes the sweet horsehide . . .
   He makes the diamond dance.

My room, my heart's all cluttered up—
   Clips, scraps, diary.
I study my gospel scorecards, pray
   And litter, order, sigh.

I hang around the stadium,
   I hang around the bars.
It's full-blown now—but can he see?—
   I am all eyes, all ears.

Annie Burns is the name I give,
   It is my baseball name,
And this diamond life is a life apart,
   and everything but tame.

It's not like where you type all day
   And never score a point.
Its home is not all up-in-the-air.
   Either you're safe or you ain't.

My story . . . I go over it
   Again and again, as if
I could make madness plain to you,
   Just plain garden stuff.

The fated field, the devil's pitch,
   The globe, its spin, the sun . . .
It's here we get a glimpse of gods.
   I'm not the only one

I know, but of all us cockeyed gals
   Glued to the diamond tilt,
I am the only one I know
   Who feels this thunderbolt

As Swat whams the apple over the fence,
   Or at any move he makes:
He shifts his feet, my belly writhes,
   All twisted up with snakes.

A diamond is a girl's best friend.
   Ha Ha—I told you so.
We were engaged at Wrigley Field.
   You are the last to know

How I was the pull behind your whack,
   My hand the one inside
Your mitt, my keen eyes on your balls . . .
   Good luck, my love, God-speed.

Some Whiz Kid, you, to ditch the Cubs
   And me, your secret Annie.
My room, my heart's still cluttered up
   With you. Why don't you die?

In the loony-bin I ponder you
  All twisted up with snakes,
Shot down—is that face mine or yours?
  I guess I've got what it takes.

I make the meaning of my life
  That night at the Edgewater Beach:
I send that note; you answer it.
  At the door, I'm about to reach

For my paring knife, but you slip past.
  I reach my gun. You say
I'm a silly honey to think of this,
  You're such a decent guy.

Point-blank. It's done, and I kneel down
  And hold your hand, your eyes.
I mess my hem in the spill of blood,
  Safe on your sacrifice.

It's here you get this glimpse of gods.
  Here come the flashbulbs, fuzz.
Annie Burns is the name I give,
  Nineteen, and why is because.

I'm finally in on your headlines, Swat,
  Closer than any wife.
That's just why I got that hotel room,
  That's why I brought the knife.

The bullet was for me, I swear.
  According to my plan,
First I'd open you, then blast
  Myself—we'd die as one.

I missed your heart by just an inch—
    How lucky—just enough
To make a miracle, beyond
    Just plain garden stuff.

I wasn't safe 'til you filled me up
    Like God fills up a saint.
The game's much like. You're in or out.
    Either you're safe or you ain't.

My diamond life may be fouled away,
    But my split-skinned heart's still fair.
Who doesn't know that Annie Burns,
    When this cursed play is over,

Will rise right up from Kankakee
    And start all over again,
With hits and catch-as-catch-can and breaks
    For home, as some light-fingered man?

Or anything, to bring me back,
    To all my fans out there
Who love to watch me, win or lose,
    My heart completely bare

In court, the way it was that day,
    And in the papers, too.
This is America—it's love
    And war and hullabaloo.

It's bang-bang plays, split-second affairs,
    Putting a spin on the globe.
It's tenderness and violence,
    All that jazz and sob . . .

My story . . . I go over it
   Again and again like a game
I put on *your* glamour with my crime.
   But I won't accept no shame.

For she's a jolly good fellow
   Who can say to passion: die.
A diamond is a girl's best friend
   That nobody can deny.

TO MAKE A DRAGON MOVE:
FROM THE DIARY OF AN ANOREXIC

It would have starved a gnat
To live so small as I—
And yet I was a living Child—
With food's necessity

Upon me like a Claw
I could no more remove
Than I could coax a leech away—
Or make a Dragon—move—

      —Emily Dickinson, No. 612

I have rules and plenty. Some things I don't touch.
I'm king of my body now. Who needs a mother—
a food machine, those miles and miles of guts?
Once upon a time, I confess, I was fat—
gross. Gross belly, gross ass, no bones
showing at all. Now I say, "No, thank you," a person
in my own right, and no poor loser. I smile
at her plate of brownies. "Make it disappear,"

she used to say, "Join the clean plate club." I disappear
into my room where I have forbidden her to touch
anything. I was a first grade princess once. I smile
to think how those chubby pinks used to please my mother.
And now that I am, Dear Diary, a sort of magical person,
she can't see. My rules. Even here I don't pour out my guts.
Rules. The writing's slow, but like picking a bone,
satisfying, and it doesn't make you fat.

Like, I mean, what would *I* want with a fat
Diary! Ha ha. But I don't want you to disappear
either. It's tricky. "Form in a poem is like the bones

in a body," my teacher says. (I wish he wouldn't touch
me—ugh!—he has B.O.—and if I had the guts
I'd send him a memo about it, and about his smile.
Sucking the chalk like he does, he's like a person
with leprosy.) I'm too sensitive, so says Mother.

She thinks Mr. Crapsie's Valentino. If my so-called mother
is getting it on with him behind my back, that fat
cow . . . What would he see in her? Maybe he likes a person
to have boobs like shivery jello. Does he want to disappear
between thighs like tapioca? His chalky smile
would put a frosting on her Iced Raspberry, his "bone"
(another word for IT, Sue said) would stick in her gut,
maybe, bitten right off! Now why did I have to touch

on that gross theme again, when I meant to touch
on "thoughts too deep for tears," and not my mother.
That Immortality thing, now—I just have a gut
reaction to poems like that—no "verbal fat"
in poems like that, or in "the foul rag and bone
shop of the heart." My God! How does a person
learn to write like that? Like they just open to smile
and heavy words come out. Like, I just *disappear*

beside that stuff. I guess that's what I want: to disappear.
That's pretty much what the doctor said, touching
me with his icy stethoscope, prying apart my smile
with that dry popsicle stick, and he said it to Mother.
And now all she says is "What kind of crazy person
would starve herself to death?" There I am, my gut
flipflopping at the smell of hot bread, my bone
marrow turning to hot mud as she eases the fat

glistening duck out of the microwave, the fat
swimming with sweet orange. I wish it would disappear,
that I . . . If I could just let myself suck a bone—

do bones have calories?—I wouldn't need to touch
a bite of anything else. I am so empty. My gut
must be loopy thin as spaghetti. I start to chew my smile.
Is lip-skin fattening? I know Hunger as a person
inside me, half toad, half dwarf. I try to mother

him: I rock and rock and rock him to sleep like a mother
by doing sit-ups. He leans his gargoyle head against the fat
pillow of my heart. But awake he raves, a crazy person,
turned on by my perpetual motion, by the disappearing
tricks of my body; his shaken fist tickles drool to my smile.
He nibbles my vagus nerve for attention. Behind the bone
cage of my chest, he is bad enough. He's worse in my gut
where his stamped foot means binge and puke. Don't touch

me, Hunger, Mother . . . Don't you gut my brain.
Bones are my sovereigns now, I can touch them here and here.
I am a pure person, magic, revealed as I disappear
into my final fat-free smile, where there is no pain.

THE WIVES OF WATERGATE   *for my father*

I don't know *what happened. I am just telling you what everybody*
thinks *happened, what* might *have happened, what you* are saying
happened. If that is history, I am telling you history.

—*Rose Mary Woods*

The Account: Martha Mitchell

I love its gentle warble
I love its gentle flow
I love to wind my tongue up
And I love to let it go.

—1937 Pine Bluff High School
   Yearbook, captioning Martha Beall's
   picture

No, I didn't want to go to town
like we did . . . for God knows what . . . election.
But then, there were the perks and parties thrown
for us, and how many gals have the FBI
around to iron their gowns and zip them up?
One day I marched with the Salvation Army.
I organized the Cabinet wives and cut down
those dumb old oaks so John could have a longer
view from the Attorney General's office. I hope
I improved things, and then of course I had to
say what I thought, and I thought truth was stronger
than protocol. John called me his unguided
missile. I told the press John was my favorite hero

The Account was Martha Mitchell's code name in the Nixon Administration.

in all history. I let my mouth go to my head.
But I'll have you know my heart was in it too.

I'm from the South and marriage is more important
to me than politics. Let me let you in
on a secret: Richard Nixon stole my husband,
warped his ear and heart. It wasn't any fun
anymore to be wife of the top cop in the game.
There was a fishy fume in Washington.

They thought I was a bubblehead, that crime
was something I didn't understand, and then . . .

I guess I knew too much for a party girl.
The secrets . . . shut up, Martha . . . issued rank.
Sure, I went through John's briefcase—I can tell
some heat from a burn. I listen in. A wife must know
what her man is up to. Mine just didn't think.
He sold his soul. And I? I should have said no.

There's nothing wrong with America—except
the little jerks, the hooligans that try
to run the show. And *she* is none too apt—
yes, I mean the so-called first lady
snubbing me like I didn't know baked wind
from blowing wise.
                     I've never analyzed
what a Cabinet wife is, so I've just remained
Martha—the country needs comedy—I've sized
up the Supreme Court: no youth, no women,
just nine old old men. Why don't they just abolish
it and all politicians, every goddamned one.

∽

I speak the truth and they put it out I'm a lush.
They want me to climb up the wall. O.K.—
but only as far as the writing on it. I see
what I see and I say what I saw. I am so
sick of being pitied—and *she* said Martha's
"sick," but no flowers came as far as I know.
It's not menopause. I'm going to watch the news:
I want to know how long I'm going to be
a political prisoner. When I am free
I'm going to write a book. My elephant memory
is already on tape, and let me tell you, Honey,
there will be no (expletive deleted)
secrets about those suitcases of boodle
sitting in my hall, or the way I've been treated
or Richard Nixon's . . . (unintelligible) . . .
I'm going to bring the house down, speak my mind.
It's going to sell better than *Gone With the Wind*.

I'm telling you: I am important enough
to be killed. I've waked up screaming for how
many years now . . . ? The little girl from Pine Bluff . . .
I've waked up screaming ever since California,
ever since the CREEP that I believed in
broke into the Watergate. We got the alert
at 6:30 a.m. And that was when
everything was decided. I was going to get hurt.

Up 'til then John thought my honesty
was real cute, and King Richard even said
"Give 'em Hell, Martha." They'd given me
so much of it, I had it to give. Instead
of thanks, they lock me up with thugs, wrestle
the telephone out of my hands, beat me up,
stick a needle in my ass, go and tell

the world I'm a boozer, and a loon—no hope
for Martha. Well, Martha's got her bathroom
phone, eyes, and a tongue. Has her reason.

It was filthy politics and not my man
I wanted my separation from.

And so I'm telling you like I told the *Times*
and T.V. buzzards—bastards—Richard Nixon
should resign. All those dirty leaky crimes,
and John is protecting him, the worse for John,
and now he won't speak to me—sitting in his den
like Al Capone, then sneaking out. I'd like
to throw a bottle of ink at him, right on
his bald head. Sweetheart, I'm up salt crick,
and if I'm sloshed, well, I have a reason to be:
they are trying to put me away, they open my mail,
my telephones click and pop, they killed Allende,
and they can do the same to me what with all
their Mafia buddies. Listen, if you don't hear
from me, you have them drag the East River.

That's right. I threw his goddamn clothes
right out in the hall, and I'll tell you what else:
You know that portrait of John, that fancy-puss
over the sofa?—well, I was just all bristles—
that mug—so I took it down (it took two men
to hang it, you know, but anger makes you strong),
and I dragged out the SOS pads, the turpentine,
Clorox, Ajax, mayonnaise, catsup . . . didn't take long
to scrub out the face. Then I got on the phone,
but I don't recall who I called—sometimes
I think maybe the fake Martha—you know, the one
who makes these calls and gives my name—
is me after all. Who else would be so stupid,

so hurt—I swear—but I've never been committed
to anything save John and the country's good . . .

You are talking to a jackass . . . Gullible, Honey,
you don't know how gullible Martha's been
since all this Waterjunk. What's really funny
is I'm a nonentity, a person who all of a sudden
has become a person who has no meaning—
do you know what I mean?
The Public? Shit. You are a nonentity as far
as you yourself are concerned. I'm tired of being
passed off as a lunatic. I tell myself you're
wrong, Martha. I say it hasn't happened
to you. You are dreaming it, Martha. What
I want is to be in Pine Bluff in a grave
alongside my mother, my mother who never gave
a damn. It's come to that. This is the end.
No more. I'm signing off. I don't need it.

The play's the thing: Pat Nixon

I met Richard Nixon at a play
audition—the parts we wanted I forget.
He was showing off. He caught my eye,
but I ...
   I thought he was some kind of nut.

He hung around. I fixed my roommate up
with him. That didn't work. And he would drive
me to Los Angeles, all patter and pep,
for my dates with other men—
       indicative
of great persistence, if not passion. Well.
It got to me—his singlemindedness.

Apart from me—I saw—the fugitive goal
inspired the play, and his weird ...
        stick-to-itiveness? ...
moved me finally.
     I chipped in to buy
the engagement ring. I wanted a family.

One day some guy from the Republican Party
called up. I don't know why they thought of Dick.
Other than the fact he'd voted for Dewey,
he wasn't political. Was it a joke?

It was for him ... I guess ... I don't quite know ...
like a play or kind of courtship, and all's fair

in love and ... I was in love and even though
I'd been hoarding for a house ... before

I could say "knife" our house became the House
and our life one long long run. I've been both staff
and distaff. I tire, but I never cancel out.
I go on. Sometimes I even laugh

at the way things conspire. You think you are
safe home, then someone calls. Duty is dear.

You play by ear. It chooses you, the script
of a lifetime. You do or die. Take him.
That's politics.
            I would have rather kept
myself for myself, my family.
                        I'm glum
sometimes.
            I think the greatest luxury
would be to frown for one whole day and not
touch another person, just one whole day
of anonymity ...
                free time for who knows what.

Once, in '54, I had an evening
all for myself. Could not think what I ought
to do (Dick had gone off to do something
secret), so I pressed every single suit
in his closet.

            I guess you'll laugh at that scene.

I just hate complainers. I won't complain.

~

Don't come to me now and ask about Watergate.
All I know is what I read in the press.
I know they're wrong. I know it's wrong to hate . . .

that gestures can't be all . . . hello and roses.

When you know the truth, as I do, you have nothing
to fear. I pray for the media. They're out
for the pound of flesh. There is no use crying

over what's done . . . it's politics and it

will go away. I pray. I will myself
not to be afraid or sick or bored.
I will myself to love, and I do. The wolf

is at the door, but it's an imperfect world,

so what do you want me to say? I keep right on
answering letters. Thousands. I read each one.

I answer, not for everyone, but as I can.
The play has dulled me. But I still go on.

Saving history: Rose Mary Woods

Secretaries need their sleep as much
as anyone. They need to dream they'll meet
The Man on His Way, indispensably attach
themselves to power. This is, of course, just what

happened to me. There was, as everybody
knows, an incident in '52.
All our lives were turning topsy-turvy.
I stood with Pat. I had a cloth coat, too.

I helped her with the kids. I fed the dog
most likely to change the world. And in my hand
I held the telegram to Ike—the big
gesture: resignation. Would I send

it? I would have sooner strangled Checkers.
I held on. I had hold of both our futures.

Ike liked Dick's show. Before Dick knew, he cried
backstage. He cried to me and not to Pat.
I joked with him. Just sleep on it, I said.
He did. Our dreams got bigger after that,

despite hurled stones in Caracas, the dirty
race in 1960, when such a lot
of dead Democrats were resurrected by
machine to vote for Mr. Camelot,

despite the loss of California's
governorship, and tears again, and years

in between when I and I alone was
his whole staff to comfort him, holding
on . . . We were sleeping on it, gathering
the silent majority in *their* nightmares.

I moved up as my man moved. I even
got my suite in the Watergate, and clothes
that sparkle. I have a million mementos,
doodads worth a break-in, finally. Heavens!

I'm sentimental about the man. I save
everything. People tease me about the mask
that R.N. wore one Halloween. I gave
it to the archives. The future's going to ask

But there were snakes in Paradise. For one,
Haldeman sent me a bunch of roses
that said, move down the hall, Baby. And then

for all the details. And I save the pith
of his speeches, the way he breathes between
the lines is the way I type them out, my Smith-
Corona strapped to my lap on Air Force One,

H. called me a lush. But President Nixon
remembered. I am the one he doesn't have to
finish his sentences for.

like poems, with breaks for emphasis. I have
this soap-box knack, although I only stand
behind the lines and wait . . .

I moved up again
when Haldeman got sacked for the cover-up.

~

                         but now I don't
know what to do . . . these transcripts . . . how to save
the face behind them.

Rosemary's Baby: the secret cash. Some hope.
But then, no hope. There was Rosemary's booboo.

                         I don't understand
why I must type it exactly so . . . I won't
disobey, of course. If it must be done,
it must. These Watergate words, the phone, the press,
glare and gossip, hurry please, the muck, the mess . . .
after all our work, our dreams, resignation

is unthinkable. All day with this damn
earphone, trying to put straight this patchiness
of static, whisper, expletive and hiss . . .
This is what it's come to? Said and done?

    Eighteen minutes of my typing life.
    Eighteen minutes in the oval office.
    Eighteen minutes. I have had *enough*.
    What is eighteen minutes, more or less?

I don't know what happened. I am just
telling you, I must have been half asleep.
I didn't want a single word to get lost.
So much noise over it. What I wouldn't give
for even more silence. It was a slip.
I swear. It's gone—what I tried to save.

Pay-offs: Dorothy Hunt

Nobody can tell a story like my Howard can,
spin out a plot so full of bravissimo,
keep you on the edge of the bed . . .
                                        I've been
around with him. In Montevideo,
Mexico, Tokyo, Madrid . . . (he'd haunt the moon
if paid to make snoopie there, or, comme il faut,
whoop up some lunar plot to wow the feds).

I married him, partly, for this to-and-fro,
the surprises.
                He entertains the kids
with his CIA disguises—not long ago
it was a crazy red wig. He was talking funny,
had us in stitches.
                        Of course it's touch-and-go
sometimes. (I don't trust his chum Gordon Liddy.)

Him cocksman, hero; me Jane . . . I like his fairy tales . . .

But what's this . . . ? He wants me to . . . *There is no one else?*

I don't know why I have to get mixed up . . .
You'd think that someone else could carry cash
to the Cubans. I get no perks from CREEP.
Howard can't be bothered? What's the fuss,
anyhow? What's for them to scritch about?
Whose money is it, why not checks?
                                        At first

I had a lot of questions. Then I got
inklings.
   It wasn't just pity for the cursed
Watergate burglars, who of course were only
doing something in the line of duty
like Howard's often done, to make the country
fierce against its foes . . .
       This is (hush) money
in my purse.
     The fools, I want to say, the fools!
I'll make the drop. *Since there is no one else.*

All life goes on in secret. My Howard, even you
can't keep your double-O on the one that gives it away.
I mean death—that blabbermouth, that horrid true
fixative to end all fixatives and pay—
whom you've always set your flimsy reed against, when all
is said and done. You cat around and pussyfoot it
for all you're worth (your mouth is worth) and still
something's sneaking up on you . . .
       Now why is it
I am thinking this way? I've flown an awful lot.
It's just—if this damn plane goes down—well, here am I,
huggermugger housewife with her laundered loot,
and somebody's going to wonder—who the hell am I,

and for whom do I carry all these tattletales . . . ?
For him, his stories.
     There isn't anybody else.

Sugar and spice and everything:
Tricia Nixon Cox

I do not unnecessarily smile.
I do not care to. In '68 I did
my bit. For instance, I agreed to preside
over Virginia's Azalea Festival.

(We were so scared the election would be stolen
from him the way it was in 1960.
Those evil people have always hated Daddy.
They call me the tiniest Nixon, the careful one.)

But there I was, strep throat on top of it all,
keeping going by knowing how my father
would stop the violence and all the juvenile
delinquency, remembering how to flatter:
"Oh, I just love your azaleas! Oh, I love
that birdcage! All that silver—just imagine
polishing it!" I was beside myself,
pouring out the sugar and spice, and then . . .
        WE WON.
But the campaigns are never never over.
Even after we were in the White House
I was supposed to get up early, care
about schools, mental hospitals, ghettos,
go out and show it. I did give a Masked Ball
I cared about. And that was about all.

He ordered it—seven feet of wedding cake—
for my Big Day in the world, in the Rose Garden.
I'd like to spend my life dashing that way

through flower petals to the waiting limousine,
knowing he is smiling just for me. I'd like
to be a perfect child again, smile naturally.

Then I had my own home and my china,
Blue Tree by Lenox, and Lunt's Eloquence
for silver. For a while the media
were just interested in me for slants
on young marrieds. "Love is the most important
thing," I say, "but love is so intangible."
They nod. "Cooking's arcane," I say, "I can't
do bacon just right, but I suppose I will

learn." Now there is this Watergate caper.
Humiliation never ends. And I thought Spiro
was handling the press. Accusers everywhere!
My Dresden figurines. The practiced smile.
Always in danger. Somehow I knew the evil
would win. To grow up is a real disaster.

Was somebody trying to tell me something?:
"Mo" Dean

Somehow I thought it would turn out differently.
I was ready to be a "good soldier,"
which is what you told me, John, I'd have to be
in Washington. Oh, my boy scout, honor

bright, that's what I'm trying to be—so hard.

I'm squarely behind you as you testify
right and left, my profiles being compared
by the cameramen, my ears . . .
                         Oh, Baby,
what did you say?
                    You couldn't live on credit.

(I wish I were at home with my Catherine Cookson.)

After you told them the nearly five thousand dollars
you borrowed from the White House slush fund was
to pay for our yard dirt and honeymoon.

Why couldn't you forget it, just forget?

Why did you have to go and tell the Chief,
and after we were starting to get the real good perks,
about that "cancer," and all those Watergate jerks?

It's honesty, my worry-wart, that always comes to grief.

~

And I've always tried to be spotless, change my suit
for a single speck, appear with every hair in place.
Little Mo has a knack for luxury. Disgrace
is something she can't handle.
                        Still, I sit

with my head up, calm outside. I take little
sips of ice water, freeze my lips, while Senator
Goody Baker asks you again, again what did the President
know and when did he know it . . . from you . . . where is the power
and the glory you said I would have to know how to handle
in Washington?
                    You seemed so innocent.

Resignation is not good:
Julie Nixon Eisenhower

Why me, they ask me. Well, if you want to know,
my father didn't beg me to go out and stump
the country for him. It's just . . . I get this lump
in my throat . . . at home. He paces, mumbles . . . how

do you think he feels? Constitutionally
speaking, he's in great shape—just baffled how
to put this bogus mess behind us. As you know,
he's got some tricky problems—diplomacy

abroad, and then at home he is so thoughtful—
a corsage for every prisoner of war
's mother at the banquet—and he does it all
under siege. He is deep in making the future
safe, doing what is good. Resignation is
not good. He is innocent. I believe in this.

Now I am really sorry for the press.
They seem to have this hang-up, still seem to need
me to re-assure them Daddy is
blameless. Well, he said so. Let me plead
for a little fairness. I won't concede
a single misdeed, and he won't resign unless
there's proof. I'll admit he's sad, he's off his feed,
he limps, but still—and I'm with him on this

right down the wire—the Presidency is
too magnificent a mandate. Greed
and lies and filth of all sorts . . . those

petty lackeys' faults . . . I'm petrified
to think you might believe the stories you read
in the *Washington Post*. It's . . . well, it's . . . just cockeyed.

So what would I want to read the transcripts for?
There he is—my father—working his heart
out running the country—and now he's got
to take the blame. Watergate's nothing more
than the manufacture of hateful hostile minds.
What would I want to read the transcripts for?
Working his heart out to be a great leader,
and then—behind his back—those so-called friends . . .

I was a political baby. I learned to walk
in Congress. I learned how to smile and to remember
names, to shake hands. And I learned to talk
in the Senate. When there's a decent joke I laugh.
What would I want to read the transcripts for?
Daddy laughs. If you think it hasn't been rough . . .

To live with a man who sees the worst. He sulks.
It's rough. Just think. When David had his head
shaved by the Navy, I went out and had
my curls cut off. We used to share insults,
get mad together. Now we get mad apart.
I'm on the road and he's alone at HoJo's
eating chocolate brownies, studying laws
that may have nothing to do with trust. I hurt

all over, to think of him staying up all night
to read those darn transcripts. When I get back—
the dishes in the sink, everything a mess—
I yell . . . I'm sorry. I was meant to be . . . just might . . .

if only we could jog along the Potomac
together, me in hot pants, no hassle, no press.

A caution: Katharine Graham

How did I get my power, such as it is?
I started out with everything but love.
A spoiled childhood. Where there is money enough
to go around, but hardly a goodnight kiss,
you learn . . . to look before, to test the wind,
let sleeping dogs, to see, to feel, to count
the cost . . . caution and toughness are what you want.
Don't hear your mother's praise: "Dear, you remind
me of myself." Just turn away. I learned
my father's work. I faced the empty page
and bit my lip 'til words came, and rage
at emptiness filled out some profile, sound
or not. A story done. With vultures all
around, to give up is unthinkable.

Obviously, you won't risk your whole
newspaper if you don't think that you have
something worth it. I always said that all
we were doing was a piece of investigative
reporting. There isn't any other motive.

I let some risky things go to press, but hell,
anybody who's imaginative
could have seen the writing on the wall,
at least after Woodward and Bernstein's oracle
started to spout from that deep source, to give
so much that checked out. Those three were the brave
ones. All I did was realize in full

≈

this story that was happening, was real.
If I suffered, I suffered to believe.

I prefer to keep my opinions to myself.
(For years I was a no-opinion person.)
We're not, at the *Washington Post*, god damn
it, do-gooders! We're not the big bad wolf.

Watergate? I'll tell you what it means
to me: a good story, a specific play
of specific characters. It is not the way
everything is. You don't, in the end,
tell any definitive Truth when neutrality
is your god. The awful magnitude
uncovered is no more than a prelude.
Then reflections, for each alone. Reality
is all we hope to bring to light. And after all,
it's not a moral business, not political.

MISS AMERICA COMES ACROSS
HER DAUGHTER   *for my mother*

Who do we kill, which image in the mirror, the mother, ourself,
our daughter????? Am I my mother or my daughter?

—*Anne Sexton,* Letters

'Tis that little gift called grace
Weaves a spell round form and face . . .
And if you would learn the way
How to get that gift today—
How to point the golden dart
That shall pierce the Prince's heart—
Ladies, you have but to be
Just as kind and sweet as she!

—*conclusion of Perrault's* Cinderella

I   *Beginning with the mirror*

There you are at the three-way mirror, the same
mirror I grew up in, checking left and right
profiles against each other . . .

On the one hand you see beauty, on the other beast;
and straight ahead, in plain view of the wall
and door behind you,

I stand, spied and spying on you as you make up
a not original daydream palaver, lips closing
round that kissable "no."

My reflector, my inquisitor, together you and I
are a much of a muchness, a symmetry
of symmetries

and inner mysteries, oracles and fairy tales,
and from Nancy Drew to Madison Avenue—
copies and copies sold—

retold. Ideally it is difficult to tell us
apart, while all told, together, we are
the prime time American

commercial. You are my living doll; I make you
all over in my image, teach you how to:
cross your ankles,

sit tight with a tiny teacup on your knee; play
fair at hopscotch, dibs and Sunday school
picnics; eschew hangnails,

babyfat and fast boys; take bubble baths, wish
on star light star bright, pediddles, dandelion
seeds puffed to air;

use lipstick, white lies, charm and embroidery;
be well-dissembled in the eyes of the fathers;
posture, posture . . .

Now how glad you must be that I made you slave
in beauty's Siberia from twelve to seventeen, live
that loser-to-looker cliché

that made me, crowned me half my life ago,
your superlative average Miss America:
five foot six

one hundred and eighteen thirty-five twenty-three
thirty-four golden hair blue eyes
that have seen the glory:

the perfect distillation of pride and pain and magic
potions, an Alice who has eaten her way
to the perfect size;

that impostor Goldilocks with her spiritual hair
at home when she's lost, that connoisseur-of-beds
consumer from nowhere;

Psyche hard pressed to Eros' arrow, engaged in unrelenting
search from alligator farms to war zones,
from county fairs to teamsters'

conventions, singing "God Bless America," launching
Mickey Mouse balloons, kissing tame bears;
the little engine

that could, and did. And now, by the mother-daughter-
holy ghost of poise, by diet and deep knee bend
will you also worship

our shape of success, the hourglass figure with its three
minutes of talent, and all the fairy tales will
fall right into place

behind you, shining white pebbles to show you home.

II *She walks; she talks*

It sounds so easy. Mother may I? Step-hop-jump?
No, you may not. Glide this way in baby steps
as queens must do

in swimsuit and evening gown. See how I walk on air,
twinkle by, disguise the fact that the human gait is a chain
of interrupted falls . . .

Meanwhile learn to breathe: it must come from your gut.
When you're sure you're alone, go: hah hah hah hah hah
and pant and snort like a horse.

That's it, and then you catch yourself up on your toes,
brush knee over knee to smooth the uncouth bounce,
eliminate all space

between your thighs, and, presto! You're a mermaid
on a unicycle. Be sure to think of bubbles,
diamonds, Tinkerbell

and poodle puppies. Your eyes must be the exclamation points
on every utterance, your lips slide like electric doors
over your well greased teeth.

And train that heft of voice on fairy tales out loud
as if to a child; inject the expectant swag and savvy
you do not necessarily feel . . .

And whether you're mincing with feet or words, be familiar
with forest spirits and wry amphibians with powers
and a king's hand to give.

Then amid gleams and silver linings, ogres, killed and thrilling,
be up in the air with an orphan's wink, with beauty
waking, as if you care

to come across a happy ever after. Impress your life
on your judges, tell them Daniel Boone and Pocahontas
hang in your family tree.

I said that I watered my prize-winning 4-H turnips
with vodka and grape pop, that I began to be pretty
when I began reciting

the Lord's Prayer backwards in the tub, that the X-rays
showed a perfect tooth in my left ovary,
that I raised snakes

to practice motherhood. Anything you say is true
enough. And they'll begin to see Her in you—
scintillating fragments

bundled in an infinitely pedestrian versatility.
The secret is: you do not have to be born to be
Miss America.

In the duties of our identity there is only She, no me, no you.

III   *Lessons in thresholds, smiles, and talent*

To get on, Miss America must know threshholds,
how to urge an entranceway out of thin air,
swish through with the formidable

effect of a trained leopard threading a flaming hoop,
as if the audience were not a forest of evil eyes.
She must smile

at the perfect pitchdark, as if unblinded by the glare.
Greet the blankness warmly, like an old old friend.
This will be the same smile

we've practiced, remember, between us and the mirror,
rehearsed at walls, mailboxes, closed doors, dust
mice, moving vans, stones.

This smile is a private threshold crossed in public,
a drama-thing, and nothing lost . . .
Talent? Well, it's true

you never learned to sing or dance or play the accordion,
to paint a face that wasn't yours, yodel, prestidigitate . . .
but you might do

a speech on how to pack a picnic hamper, or recite
"The Spider and the Fly." Why not accompany yourself
(with one easy lesson or two)

on the marimba or vibraharp? Or dress as Betsy Ross
and whistle "The Stars and Stripes" on roller skates.
How about a home movie

of you and your trained cat? In three minutes
you want to come across as something special,
but not too serious.

Despite the lewd things under stones, the wolves,
the blue beards, the Avon lady so late at night
with her basket of apples . . .

Believe in dazzle, Dear, and in spite.

IV   *Entre nous: lesson approaching congeniality*

If I seem to put you down, it is just so you can be
fulfilled by the Cinderella formula: abasement first.
From ashes to exodus,

through grief and jealousy—it happens with all
who are to be queens—and from victim to
the perfect fit

of a slipper, or all the dresses in the land of Oz,
through waiting and dreams, sit tight, play fair.
Fairest? Let there be no

excess, no excelling; let none of us be original
in the sin of our dread of being without
our mutual reflections;

let each one behold in the Chosen One Herself;
be kind to frogs, accept the rose from the beast's hedge.
Worthless unto rescue,

open no forbidden chambers to see what happens
when the honeymoon is over: no simple massacre
of the former brides' bodies

but an interminable bridge game played by ghosts
of former brides grown fat and slack,
envy in their bids and bets

on who will next come through the door, discover them, join in.
Is this what Psyche saw when she went down?
Make no mistake.

Sisters and queens, Cinderellas shod for daily grace,
snug in our vestal skins and chants: mirror, mirror,
my identity, my enemy,

on the wall or off it, up against it, who is looking
fair now, who is looking more so, who is looking
at you now, or harder,

best-beloved? Make no mistake. Don't ask, I tell
myself, and now tell you. You are my second
lifetime; extend yourself

and close my circle. Do not try to cut through
the mother-knot, the Gordian macramé, wordless net
I use to package you . . .

Imagine the high wire tensed from womb to womb. There
our images toe toward each other, dance mid-air.
Let most things be

beneath you, even, at times, congeniality. At times
I've slapped your face. I have the right to be
mistress of your ceremonies,

I've been here before. I kissed the first words
into your mouth: please and thankyou, no
and thankyou, please,

but no, I love you, only . . . congeniality is not
what we're here for. You smile magnolias; this glass
goblet framed by our tête-à-tête

depends on these chins we've firmed by exercise, mouth stretched
to scream, puckered to kiss, learning the mean expression . . .
Now, how separate

the two. From one queen to the next, what is most true
and what is most made up is this: illusion:
this breakable glass, this cup

of light between shadows, eye to eye and lip to lip.

MADEIRA'S HEADMISTRESS   *for Elizabeth Hadas*

Would you please tell the jury what you meant on March 10 when
you said, "I was a person and no one ever knew." —Joel Aurnou,
lawyer for the defense of Jean Harris, accused of killing Dr.
Herman Tarnower (author of The Complete Scarsdale Medical
Diet) *on March 10, 1980*

I was a person sitting in an empty chair. —Jean Harris

I   *The madness*

At Madeira they learn to be tasteful, ladylike,
to save their bodies, conceal them, let them be,
to act as if . . . as if there were something there
and not there. Ideally, I should have been
single—a widow, spinster, divorcee.
Now all seem apt to me, though mistress was
apter for fourteen years. The afternoon
I left my position at the school, I spent
putting my will in order, kissing my dogs
goodbye, test-firing on the terrace. I planned
to do it by his pond where daffodils
would ease the shock. I drove five hours with flowers
and ammunition. I called him from the stairs.
I had the gun, the flowers, the best intent
in the world to have our last words be most kind.
Then I found her green-blue satin negligee
in my bathroom. I flung it on the floor.
He didn't follow my script. I heard the glass
shatter as the curlers hit the window.
He hit me. I went and smashed the mirror. Again,

he hit me. I turned the same sore cheek again.
He turned away. I put the gun to my head.
He grabbed. His hand was shot. I stood and stared.
I got the gun. He lunged and I fell back.
I felt a muzzle hard, pressed to my stomach.
We were closer than love, I squeezed the trigger
and felt no pain, but he was on the floor.
I clicked the gun against my head, then fired
through air; again, it clicked against my head,
empty, broken. I helped him back to bed
and left him, fled, came back, and he was dead.

II   *The letter*

I never should have mailed my shriek of pain.
I had to expel those girls. It was a mess.
To think of him with that adulteress,
that psychotic slut of his . . . Insane
of him. Here's something I cannot explain:
Hi was a snob. You'd think that his mistress
would not be tawdry, coarse. How could he kiss
us interchangeably? She put a stain
on my nightgown, bright orange. My yellow dress
I found balled up and smeared with feces, yes,
human shit. And he could live with this.
He wanted fun and games and happiness
and my distress was tactless to excess
perhaps. But I am not a murderess.

III   *The logic*

If murder's misdirected suicide
and theft is inverse gift—you take from her
to whom you'd promise love or payment, were

you not unequal—then I'm satisfied
to say I killed myself in him, where pride
had fallen first; to say he robbed my store
of dignity, but he was the bestower
in prizing it. Believe me, I'd have died . . .
All I wanted was to be beside
him, noticed, cherished, intrinsic, sanctified
not by God, but society, allied.
I am a woman, always qualified
by hemstitch and hormone, now a homicide,
but not by reason; by reason, a suicide.

IV *The spirit*

The evidence is laid before you here,
my madness, my letter, my logic, the scrutiny
of the body, every bloody particular:
positions and displacements. Now this body,
this gathering of awe and doubt, of peers
and words . . . There are too many words! Nobody
seems to notice I am not here, in tears,
at all. The woman in a pretty dress
is nowhere; headmistress and mistress though
I've acted, I'm not here, and never was.
Trim as any wife in Scarsdale, I
kept my body. I rewrote his damn book
so it wouldn't sound so cheap. To be
Somebody with *some* body—what it took
from me means nothing, but suggests a way
of being. Alone. See, I was just some *body*,
in a pretty dress, of opinions, in a play
I wrote, but no one followed. Can you see?
Of course I know this trial's about a *body*.
Mine wasn't there, the one that was, was his.
Beside it just a woman in a pretty

dress, a pretty fix, a headmistress
strayed, a lady, lady, lady, lady . . .

I am a person in an empty chair.
Let this body convict me. I was there
in spirit, and even that will disappear
before my sentence ends, before I care . . .

RINGLING BROS. PRESENT:
THE LUCKY LUCIE LAMORT   *for Chi*

Between this dreamjunk wasteland and the Milky Way, I taunt
balance, flaunt it, Lucky Lucie Lamort, Lightbody's
daughter, tiniest funambulist, star of the rag front,
topmost spangles, yeah.

Aren't you stunned by the fine panache
of a life so perfect, so glittery, so up in the air?
Steady as she goes, I love to harp on the hanging threads
of dear faint hearts, my eye on the faithful end
of my own rope, their eyes delivering the quicksilver
energy of their qualms. I boggle, abash, obsess, appall.
I totter to tease . . .
Then, all those indrawn breaths below, that suck of awe
before the fall—not quite—the vibrant adrenalines
in tune, and finally the riot panic of applause,
my extreme unction, yeah.

How I do love the tension of all stretched things:
filaments and wings, the strands and riggings
of the body, the brash fibre of a plucked string.
I dance on pure nerve, live by the corners of my eyes,
by the percipience of my footsole. I am a dazzle machine;
each sequin on me deflects the arrows the stars flick down.
I too am a heavenly body, yeah.

Does my calm repel? Defy? I outgame God and Gravity,
those old hags knitting galaxies. I sit in their spacious laps,
a nonesuch, my moxie a law to myself one hundred feet above
contradiction, that dumb mud that undoes me.
It's neck or nothing, yeah.

～

How I do love the straightest and narrowest:
I stroll, I spin and trot, I somersault;
I pirouette like Napoleon's pet between the towers
of Notre Dame, where angels fear and gargoyles gape.
I span the volcano's crater in my heatproof suit;
highfalutin as Blondin, I do the useless with *élan*,
a dare-angel married to Damocles sword whose stainless
blade I lick clean, yeah.

But on the ground you wouldn't know me at all.
At the touch of old Adam's clay my toes curl up.
I'm nullified by fundament, an invalid, a jellyfish.
What a predicament, yeah.

There was a time I loved the scuff of sawdust and paper trash.
I knew sidewalks, paths through forests, rooms and trains.
Then it happened: I could no longer touch the wide ways
of the world; beneath my knowing feet I felt the mantle
slide, too much to know, and so reboundless, such a drowse
of thumpings, criss-crossed with a disarray
of footings, so untidy; its touch a fatal threat
to the wiring of my gut, yeah.

What relief, to shinny up the guy, step out on bounce.
I find no falter here where nothing mothers me.
There is nothing like this loneliness, beyond all love.
I walk my rope-long sentences to the turning points.
At every turn my body tangles with eternity;
at every step, anew, I learn my center, feel my life
a pattern in the current and living web of all.
It is a marriage of letting go and holding on,
a balance of concentration and release, a deepest music
undulating from my toe. It is mathematical, death's friend,
immense, immense . . .

~

What a weight is the universe! What a caucus
of butterflies and whales, of nebulas and holes.
I put my slipper on its nerve and it answers me
in centimeters, spring and fall, in glitters
at the corners of my eyes, in certain longing
to leave my senses altogether, depart the wire and even air,
rise endlessly and swift to walk the summit
of the solar wind, tramp the rigging
between worlds . . .

I walk the starlight between galaxies, ride
those spinning tops with my heel; I glide
light years to God's labyrinthine ear
like a pure and dizzy prayer.
Yeah.

PATTY HEARST:
VERSIONS OF HER STORY

The genuine writer of fairy tales is a seer of the future.
(With time, history must become a fairy tale— it will become
once again what it was at its inception.)   —Novalis

This confabulation is designed for six female voices, as follows:

THE FAIRY GODMOTHER   (Fabula Grunt)

THE MOTHER   (The Queen)

THE GIRLFRIEND   (Tania-in-Waiting)

THE COMRADE   (Emily; Yolanda)

THE REPORTER

THE JUROR   (The Housewife)

THE FAIRY GODMOTHER:

Once upon a time in Storyland
one could become a king by answering
the riddle of the Mother Tongues.
In one of its hearings it goes like this:
  in sleep in waking
  in black in white
  in worlds in words
  in flower in fall
  in any balances left to right
  what are the People wanting after all?

THE MOTHER:

Once upon a time
in California, a land where melons grew
big as moons, there lived a man
who had the knack
of turning paper into bullion
by printing words on it, both front and back,
because he knew
what people wanted more than anything
was story after story after all
about what they might be or become; the People
made this cunning man a king.

THE GIRLFRIEND:

Let me take you to the wild wild West,
    a never-never land of stars and violence
        and wishes, where the very strangest
things could happen, and where there lived, once
    upon a time, a princess and her best
        friend. There was almost no difference . . .

THE COMRADE (Emily):

Once upon a time in a little town
in the country of Liberty
there lived a little girl named Emily.
She liked to dress up as a princess
sometimes, sometimes like Pocahontas,
sometimes like Joan
of Arc in her fiery passion . . .

THE COMRADE (Yolanda):

Bullshit! Let me tell you, for a hell of a
long time in this fucked-up world,
this blot on the earth called Amerikkka,
there was this class of white asshole oppressors
and then there was these masses
of fine poor people robbed blind by the soul-
fucking government, mostly black and mostly in jail,
and these people,
The People, man, were just waiting . . .

THE REPORTER:

But in the Here and Now, in the land of Media Major, the main
thing is its citizens need to devour some newspaper stories with their
daily bread and multiple vitamins. There is a kind of king there, the
King of Ink and Air, and he owns all the stories. (We call him
Randy.)

THE JUROR:

To go back: Once upon a time in America, the land of the Brave and
the Free, there lived a housewife, a perfectly ordinary housewife who
always would be reading a good book with a good old-fashioned
love story in it.

THE MOTHER:

The king took a wife, pretty as a magnolia
and smart as a tycoon's cufflinks, a summa

cum laude of taste. Their five daughters grew
in time to the tick of their grandfather's clock
and the tock of coins dropped through
the backslits of their piggy banks; their lives
were regular as please and thank you,
the click open and shut of a doll's eyes.
They loved their memories as they grew just like
the pictures in a heavy storybook,
even when these showed a giant or bicephalous
dragon carrying off a princess.

THE FAIRY GODMOTHER:

Now in the great storehouse
of the Mother Tongues was a file of precious
Old Scripts, attended by a special class
of fairy godmothers who would choose
a script that needed to be updated, dust it off,
and bestow it at the christening of some
mortal child. Thus endowed or encum-
bered, the child would bring its new life
to the old tale, its happiness, its grief . . .

Most fairy godmothers were too scrupulous
to present a story with its proper end unknown,
but some fairy godmothers were more capricious.
A successful refurbishment of a fragment
might lead to the rank of Mother Tongue
(a rank without hunger, like none
on the earth's vast fundament).

THE MOTHER:

One of the queen's daughters was named Patty,
and mine is the story of how she came
to visit a nether world, and how she came
to swallow there some terrible seed...
But until she was nineteen going on twenty
and about to be married
she seemed to be nothing special—
not even her mother could tell...

THE GIRLFRIEND:

... between them; the princess and her best friend
    were closer than sisters, close as crossed fingers,
        brave as Nancy Drew, bright as Mouseketeers,
at home in a game of Let's Pretend.

THE REPORTER:

Entre nous, I am one of the few women in Media Major's Retinue of
Report. The legmen don't like to give credit, but I have got a snout
like a pig's for the rare ramification, the ugly truffle worth its weight
in radium ... I also have legs.

THE COMRADE (Yolanda):

Then in Amerikkka, even with its slop-swilling
imperialists with their fucking fat thumbs stuck in

the money pie, there began to be something cooking
in an underground kitchen . . .

THE JUROR:

The housewife was always the last to hear what everybody was so
excited about. Like Watergate. It was all over the bridge before she
could look up the word *impeach* in *The Joy of Cooking*.

THE FAIRY GODMOTHER:

Fabula Grunt, ambitious as fairy godmothers go,
was a connoisseur of enchantments that cause
one person to become another. There was this:
The Spell of Black White and Red. Although
it seemed to be your regular abduction-of-the-princess tale,
all she knew about the spell itself was
that it involved a little ebony locket, a piece of red glass,
ruby-deep and jagged, and an ivory spindle.
Though she might have chosen any christening
at which to bestow it, she was aware of a certain king
who, in black and white, had used the word *fairy tale*
to refer to a lie; she became the invisible
presence at his daughter's christening.

THE GIRLFRIEND:

The princess and her best friend read straight through
Little Women, Heidi, and *The Five Peppers and How They Grew*
so they learned all about being very poor,
and sometimes they liked to pretend they were.

THE MOTHER:

And then one day the princess firmly said
to the king and queen the time had come for her
to leave the parental palace. Not all the silver
mines and orange groves, pools and fountains,
promises, etiquette, wonder,
blind trusts and dividends, or miles of mountains
in the world could turn her head . . .

THE GIRLFRIEND:

How resourceful they would be, how adept,
with hand-me-downs and cabbage soup, rapt
over the smallest scrap of velvet ribbon.
They would give hand-made Christmas presents to each other:
a pomander or a pincushion.
What fun!

THE MOTHER:

. . . She learned to smile
not only for the Shah of Iran, Prince Charles
or Howard Hughes, but for anyone.

THE JUROR:

Sometimes in America somebody broke a law. Then they would have
a jury of common people to hear and decide whether or not the one
accused really did it. It was like a sweepstakes whether you would
get picked for a jury or not. The housewife knew this from eighth

grade Civics, everyone did, but she was surprised anyhow when that jury duty thingy came in her mailbox. (She hardly ever got first class type mail.) She thought about checking the box to get out of it because of being a woman, but then she remembered Perry Mason and thought she would just go and see. She felt a little thrill, like at the dentist's sometimes, when the novocaine goes straight to your stomach. She was wanted.

THE COMRADE (Emily):

Emily had learned the games of the ruling class:
school and cops and robbers, Monopoly, Scrabble and chess;
she led cheers and marched with pride
in every Memorial Day or Fourth of July parade.
One Halloween she dressed as Betsy Ross.
In this vast land where Emily learned her liberties . . .

THE GIRLFRIEND:

The two of them read newspapers for the same reasons
they'd read fairy tales. Ann Landers, the social pages,
horoscopes so full of giggles and bewares . . . They
whispered of love and violence, almost knowing
the world was full of treachery . . .

THE COMRADE (Yolanda):

. . . a fucking blackbird pie, for instance,
ready to sing the Internationale, cool blue soul
and volcanic rock all . . .

THE COMRADE (Emily):

. . . it was all romance then.
She wanted to be an astronomer or veterinarian;
she wanted horses to love her and need her,
she wanted to be the first person to discover
a comet, like Maria Mitchell . . .

THE GIRLFRIEND:

Among the newspaper items that pleased their eyes
was the smiling announcement of the princess' engagement;
they read not a word about the odd Symbionese
Liberation Army, or what it meant . . .

THE COMRADE (Yolanda):

. . . coming up from way the hell
underground, where the future was beginning to be alive and well.
Deep in the dungeons of the fascist state,
the extent of the crime against the People
was pissing off a lot of folks, both black and white.

THE COMRADE (Emily):

Then one day when little Emily
was about as grown up as she was ever likely to be,
she found herself transfixed at her vanity.

THE REPORTER:

But to tell you the truth, I am still composing these saditorials in my head about the various women drenched in the leaks of Watergate when that Marcus Foster story breaks:

THE COMRADE (Emily):

Here she had sat humming the Miss America theme song, sighed over "Just the Way You Look Tonight," and "Here Comes the Bride."

THE MOTHER:

The princess didn't have any quarrels with the way
her father helped to run the world, didn't want to get away
from that, didn't want to go and be a movie star.
It was simply that she had fallen
in love, an ordinary person with an ordinary person
and she wanted to live with him. Her mother
did not entirely approve,
but let her daughter go for love.

THE REPORTER:

. . . this A-number-1 black school superintendent is wasted with a cyanide-laced bullet by this freak outfit calling themselves the Symbionese Liberation Army.

THE COMRADE (Emily):

Now all she could hear was her own
heart. She stared until the mirror began to darken

at the edges, like a death announcement
or Magna Carta parchment.

THE GIRLFRIEND:

When the princess found her older man of twenty-three
and turned from teacher's pet into paramour,
her best friend was far too curious to be
jealous. The two girls needed to taste each other's
secrets—sad, mad, or whatever—
the way monkeys need to taste each other's fleas . . .
He was common as the square root of one,
but charming and bright as a dandelion.
The friend-in-waiting would be maid of honor
and naturally catch the bouquet—what happened to one
was supposed to happen to the other.

THE COMRADE (Emily):

Emily sat and stared through her face in her mirror—
a scrim with strong light behind it—shadows there
moved and she moved with them, entering her own eyes,
following, following counter-clockwise.
It felt like reading backwards, a great undoing.
Then she was inside the vessels that fed
her vision and all she saw was red . . .
What was she seeing? Was she reliving
her own birth?

THE COMRADE (Yolanda):

Cell by cell, the embryo of the People's Army
    grew where every goddamn lily

           white capitalist hand
was smeared with filthy lucre.
                    The situation had got
so fucking crude
some children of these white turds were
                    waking up to it.
Nine of these, four young men with ideals
and five chicks who had their shit
                    together
                    found the center
of a new consciousness in this dude
          Cinque Mtume, black and beautiful
          and *bad*. He knew them prisons from
his insides out, escaped, and very
          wanted at the moment. As Fifth Prophet
he spoke to the People: "My People,
     the only way you will
          regain your freedom is to fight;
     the only way you will
          keep your guns is to use them . . ."

THE REPORTER:

So this so-called Symbionese Liberation Army sends out their own
press releases, crashing the Gates of Gazette, giving the Public
Mouth a taste of the insane. It is a story, sick, but a story nonethe-
less and a bone for the rumoregiment to pick.

THE JUROR:

When the housewife got to the courthouse and saw all the other
people that had been called to serve she knew they would never pick
her because she didn't know beans about what they asked her. And

then it turned out she was just the ticket, somebody with no clutter in their mind. When the Judge explained what "sequestered" meant, she thought briefly of her husband; he wasn't going to like it. But she went home and packed her bag and left her husband a note on the refrigerator door. She took some books along, some Harlequin, some Silhouette.

THE GIRLFRIEND:

One day the princess told her best friend she felt odd.
She had dreamed of a white balloon in the shape of a pig;
it looked pink because it was swollen with blood.
A black butterfly with a white stripe on its wings
kissed (or bit) the pig in its belly and the blood
gushed out. The butterfly could not fly away
because its paperthin wings were drenched with blood . . .

THE COMRADE (Emily):

No, it was not personal, this red.
Emily felt a wider pulse; her blood
as it marched meant
something far and away. In the inspiration
there was giving and taking, joy and lament.
She saw to the heart: all people, one
body . . .

THE GIRLFRIEND:

The princess was scared and didn't know why.
The friends felt they were on opposite sides of a deep gulley.
What did it mean? Had someone died?

All they could do was wave at each other, sadly,
each from her baffled side.

THE COMRADE (Emily):

. . . So Emily went in search and met a man
who had seen the same. To the pulse of one body
they marched down the aisle
and went out to look for the People.
They went in search of the real
People in themselves.

THE COMRADE (Yolanda):

Cinque Mtume had named his own
   self in prison, and now he named
      his freedom fighters so they was free
         of their old piggy identities.
He named them all: Bo and Osi and Cujo
         (no longer Joe and Russ and William),
         Fahizah, Gelina, Gabi and Zoya-Mismoon
         (no longer Nancy, Angela, Camilla, Pat).
Then came Emily and Bill to be Yolanda and Teko.
They all got a drop of blood now in their eye
   reddening the moon; every single one
      was one another.

THE FAIRY GODMOTHER:

When the Princess Patricia Campbell Hearst's picture
appeared on the social page in her father's newspaper
Fabula Grunt woke up and began
to recognize an oddness in the air:
a spell that she was responsible for
was about to be cast or broken.
She looked into the goblet she used for gazing
and saw clearly, felt the razor slicing
around the margin, separating the smiling
Princess' image from the surrounding
society. One black hand and one white
held the article to be read to the light.
She felt a plummet inside her from heart to heel,
like a golden ball dropped darkly into a well:
   a sure sign
  a story was about to begin
   its ends.

THE COMRADE (Yolanda):

Pig bitch out of oink by hog-it-all—
it's written all over her smug mug.
She don't even know she needs to be
fucking liberated from her mucky money sty
and get conscious, like . . .

THE FAIRY GODMOTHER:

One night a loud rude knock on the door.
It was like being jabbed in the liver
by a broomstick. The princess felt fear,
and so did her fairy godmother.

THE REPORTER:

I just happen to be hanging around the front office to do the Q-and-A
number on a sad round-up of street sisters (special for the slush
page) and this call comes in: the daughter of good King Randy has
been, no less, abducted. Just like that. Before either she or her lovey-
dove can say, "And that's the way it is, February 4, 1974," three
bodysnatchers—two male, one, alas, female—jump in with pointed
guns. There is the princess, Patty Hearst, in nothing but her blue I.
Magnin terrycloth bathrobe (petticoat-interest). And there is her
dumb fiancé who opened the door, fisted and kicked to the floor. So
they drag this girl blindfolded, half-gagged, hog-tied, screaming out
the door, cram-slam her in the trunk of this old white Chevy and
just skreel away . . .

THE MOTHER:

The queen was beside herself.
Her rage might have raised the Dead Sea.
She had let her daughter go for love.
Now this.
She wondered what the ransom would be.

THE GIRLFRIEND:

When the princess' best friend heard
   she pinched her eyes tight as a snare
     and saw it happening to her:
and I felt this shiver like a hummingbird
   poised with its needle-beak
     at my heart's cleft; I felt
the knock, the suck of the door
   opening . . . my life will be changed
     forever . . .

THE JUROR:

The housewife was thinking a lot about this Patty—rich people
didn't always have it so easy—and how on the night of the kidnap
she had fixed noodle soup from a can just like an ordinary person.
Plus she had her nice art books, her cookbooks; she liked to make
a soufflé. But, God knows, she might have wanted a little adventure.
Here she was, engaged to a nice young man . . . The housewife felt
a pang for Patty's mother, sitting there in the courtroom with her
perfect hair.

THE FAIRY GODMOTHER:

Done: the princess carried off by the light
of the full moon and stuffed in a closet.
But once it happened Fabula felt sorry about it.

~

The princess, beside herself, curled
like an unborn thing in her briny blindfold
soaked as seaweed. Meanwhile she could hear
on the other side of the door
unintelligible thumpings, laughter
tense as a crouched cat. Her brain was a tangle
of umbilicals, each spieling off to an old image—
wreckage now, more of a puzzle
than wonderland, flakes of mica in mud.
Sometimes her captors battered
her touchy ears with loud radio music
so she could not catch the swap of their talk.
A bubble of vomit stung her throat;
a scream was tucked under the root
of her tongue . . . Then someone would come
to the door to shout . . .

THE COMRADE (Emily):

The Old Emily in the New Yolanda sometimes sat up,
yawned, felt pretty, yearned for a Baskin-Robbins banana
split, a spree in a boutique . . .
And then she remembered Cinque
naming the seven virtues
    of the Cobra that would reign in the utopia
        of the Symbionese Nation: self-reliance, work for the public
            good, co-operation, responsibility, productivity, hope.
Symbiosis: getting it on together.

THE COMRADE (Yolanda):

People can fucking *change* . . . because Somebody,
   man, the secret Everybody,
      the *People*, the People's Army
raising the general *consciousness*
   like, through *struggle*—personal, public, selfless . . .
Screw Baskin-Robbins! You've got a *vision.*

THE GIRLFRIEND:

And the friend-in-waiting mused secretly
how it's kind of exciting, too, to be
the maiden in distress for real . . .
remember how in every book
Nancy gets locked up and rescued in the nick
of time?
         They'll ask some fabulous ransom,
         Dad will pay, I'll
         have some
story to tell . . .

THE REPORTER:

   For the king's sake we keep the story on ice . . . but then this jumps
   the Gates like a shot president: I quote:

Symbionese Liberation Army
Western Regional Adult Army
Communique #3, February 4, 1974

SUBJECT: *Prisoner of War*
TARGET: *Patricia Campbell Hearst—daughter of Randolph A. Hearst, corporate enemy of the People.*
WARRANT ORDER: *Arrest and protective custody; and if resistance, execution.*
WARRANT ISSUED BY: *The Court of the People.*

On the afore stated date, combat elements of the United Federated Forces of the Symbionese Liberation Army armed with cyanide loaded weapons served an arrest warrant . . .

We print it right or wrong, and it is truly done.

THE COMRADE (Yolanda):

Yolanda did push-ups, cleaned her submachine gun.

THE JUROR:

The housewife and the princess sat where they could see each other in the courtroom, but the housewife looked at the princess.

THE FAIRY GODMOTHER:

And Fabula regretted the ropes strangling
her godchild's wrists, the thick fist
of rags on her tongue, the dirty taste
of defilement, how she had to bend double

between the wall and wall and wall
and locked door that led to nothing.
A thing in a box, a riddle,
a bestowal so rash.

THE REPORTER:

Terrorists, plain but not simple. They get the poor kid's voice on a
tape, box it and send it through the Gates to the Public Mouth. Myself, I worry it like a dog:

> *"I am here because I am a member of a ruling class family . . .*
> *The SLA has declared war against the government and it's*
> *important that you . . . realize that this is not considered by*
> *them to be just a simple kidnapping . . ."*

Not simple, incredible. The ransom: seventy dollars in groceries,
and not junk food either, for each poor person in Media Major. As
if they didn't know that hunger is forever.

THE COMRADE (Yolanda):

Her being their prisoner of a war,
the victorious SLA had to keep her
in the People's Prison which, unfortunately,
had to be a closet in their safehouse, see.
But they was going to treat her just like the Geneva
Convention. They gave her a pillow. When she was a
good girl, they tied her rich bitch little hands
in front instead of in back. When she understands
to say "I gotta go pee" instead of her prim
fucking upper class "May I go to the bathroom,"
they lead her to the can.

THE JUROR:

Meanwhile the natty lawyers and the big-word doctors that can read minds and so forth were talking and talking. "Diagnosis: traumatic neurosis, acute and chronic, with dissociative features . . ." The house-wife's sister had a case of nerves, and she sure knew acute from chronic what with piles, but what was a dissociative feature?

THE FAIRY GODMOTHER:

They would lecture her at the door sometimes,
come and read firmly to her like nannies
reading the moral *Struwwelpeter* or the Grimms.
Endless drones of lies and insanities . . .

THE REPORTER:

Under ordinary circumstances, I'd be playing the bloodhound, the digger-upper. I know some croakers in the underground might mizzle me something. But I don't want to stumble on that deathnest —scoop for me and curtains for the kid. My fingers tiptoe on the keys and clues.

THE MOTHER:

The king and queen gave away food until
the giveaway turned into a throwaway.
They promised more, and money too, if only . . . but all
they got for their trouble was their daughter's unearthly

voice, trancelike in its anger, paler than eggshells,
her tongue retreating from its spellbound syllables.

THE FAIRY GODMOTHER:

The princess memorized the women's voices:
the mocks and threats and blah blah blah
of Gelina, Fahizah, Yolanda, Gabi and Zoya—
hellhags and stepsisters with grim figments for faces
and arsenic breath, the bad mothers who
finger the heart of a child in the dark,
who move to the tune of a cracked patriarch.
Finally their monotonous ravings and those of Cinque
Mtume, the driveling enchanter, let up
having exhausted her into a desperate sleep.

THE COMRADE (Yolanda):

At first she was so fucking uptight
she couldn't even shit
and they called her Marie Antoinette . . .

THE JUROR:

Back in her hotel, the housewife dreamed she was in a small dark
place, her blindfold soaked with tears, a gag in her mouth, hands tied
in back, and the worst thing of all was she had to go to the bathroom.

THE COMRADE (Yolanda):

... but when she seemed to be coming round
to the People's view of what they had in mind
they called her Tiny. She started to blend
right into the routine ...

THE JUROR:

She heard the clump of the boots, she heard a strong voice saying
her name, saying ...

THE COMRADE (Yolanda):

... She weren't so bad
as pigs go, weren't nearly half so afraid
of the dark. The Army understood ...

THE JUROR:

"You will love me with all
the hot wild passion of liberation that is in your heart." His key in
the lock was louder than the cocking of the guns ...

THE COMRADE (Yolanda):

... how horny she must be getting in the closet there,
so Cin goes and lifts her up off of the floor
by those silver dollar nipples, then just lets her

down easy and learns her the real thing.
Cujo did his thing, too, and she stopped bawling,
seemed to dig it . . .

THE JUROR:

. . . and suddenly she was awake. Her sheet was soaked and she got up and washed it so the maid of the hotel would not laugh with the other maids about it.

THE FAIRY GODMOTHER:

Fabula oversaw the dream of the princess
where she found in her prison her anger
like a fragment of Tiffany glass
smashed from a sunrise window. Its red
was deep as almost clotted blood,
a splinter of the fall's flower
with an edge, an edge for slicing away
all the cords that ever bound her
to those many things she was going to be
no longer.

THE REPORTER:

We are getting this crazy story, these communiqués with the princess talking to her father for all the world to hear:

The SLA are not the ones who are harming me . . . It's the FBI,
along with your indifference to the poor . . . Dad, I know that

you get most of the food donated . . . and you have put very
little money at all into the program . . . I have been reading a
book by George Jackson called Blood in My Eye. *I am starting*
to understand what he means when he talks about fascism in
America . . .

THE GIRLFRIEND:

The friend left behind listened hard
to the princess' message to the king.
She learned the words by heart:
"I can't believe you are doing
everything you can . . . Please listen to me . . .
I no longer seem to have any
importance as a human being . . ."

THE COMRADE (Yolanda):

Meanwhile, Tiny's old man, king
of the fascist turds, was simply not coming
fucking through, and poor people still standing
in the cold like dogs for bags of cabbages . . .

THE GIRLFRIEND:

The words on the tape stuck in the friend's throat
like a half-swallowed aspirin. She thought
to herself, with tears in her eyes:

Only in someone else's place, stories
not your own, is this feeling . . .
It does not belong to you, it is everybody's feeling,
feeling they are you, and your own feelings
are taken away . . .

THE COMRADE (Yolanda):

. . . And we say to the People:
Cry out! Cry out for all
        the millions of children of all
races who are starving and dying now and not fucking
        just cry out for the safety of one
human being.

THE FAIRY GODMOTHER:

The princess dreams under Cinque's spell.
And she finds her hunger like a sharp spindle
waiting to burst the bubble of her childhood
and leave her exposed to the dangerous need
of others. She dreams herself face to face
with the image of poverty, of the People,
each eye a red-rimmed orifice
over an endless belly distended with nothing
but a glut of sibilations. The princess
is ready, like them, to swallow anything
to still that slither and hiss.

THE COMRADE (Yolanda):

And after only about
    three months steady
of getting educated,
    the princess is ready
to come out of the closet,
    make her fucking debut
and not as some shit-
    licking deb from Hillsborough.

So they peel off the blindfold one day,
no longer sopping with bourgeois self-pity,
and call her Tania, after Che's old lady.

THE JUROR:

The housewife went over the day, doing what she was supposed to
be doing, thinking of Patty: What was it like, that moment when
the blindfold comes off her and she looks around for the one called
Cujo, that doctor's son . . .

THE COMRADE (Yolanda):

Cujo gives her this Olmec
    monkey to wear
on a string around her neck;
    Cinque gives her
a ring for her finger.

THE FAIRY GODMOTHER:

... she sees the LIGHT.
It cuts, a blade to the back of her skull
scooping a pit way back of vision, all
down her body and down to her toes she can feel
the LIGHT
before she can focus on the People,
the General and his army standing still
as riffraff astonished in a fairy tale,
and she was one of them, now and here
on the other side of the mirror.

THE JUROR:

What was that story so long ago on Sunrise Semester? The woman
has a lover she is never supposed to look at or she will be sorry, but
she can't help it, and looks, and then she is willing to do anything.
It's not the same, but the housewife thinks of it when she thinks of
love in the dark, how easy it is to love someone you can't see.

THE FAIRY GODMOTHER:

It is left only for her to dream
that she finds herself the charm
of renunciation, a little ebony locket
with a seven-mouthed cobra inside it
speaking a circle:

the world changes
the self changes the world
does not change
only the self the world changes
the self changes
the world does not change
only the self
the world changes . . .

THE MOTHER:

Then on the very first day of April,
with the blossoms just coming on the trees and all
the gardens of the palace bursting to flurries of color,
the knights of the pen received, out of thin air,
this:
> *Further communications . . . in the following*
> *seventy-two hours . . . will state city and time*
> *of release of prisoner*
>   A peony began to pulse
itself open in the queen's heart quickening.

THE REPORTER:

April fool! An awful gag in a world choked with fools, a press
jammed and all of us hanging like newborn possums on the furry
belly of words that mean nothing and everything; a teacup tempest
or a roof of gingerbread; good copy—even disappointment is news
news news when Patty says, "I have chosen to stay and fight for my

freedom and the freedom of all oppressed people." We eat it up,
blow it up; we editerrify (make it, sell it); a story made for me.

THE GIRLFRIEND:

There she is, smiling, more famous than
Miss America behind her clumsy gun . . .
She has chosen, made choice live for me;
I become Tania-in-waiting, a Red Riding Hood
perfectly at home in the wolf's belly,
a Sherwood Forest maverick, inverting good and bad.

THE MOTHER:

The peony froze behind its palings
when the distracted queen saw
the picture of her daughter, the red banner,
the seven-headed black cobra,
that smile—the queen had taught her
that smile—had it ever been false before?
The name Tania scorched her
tongue like a seed of pepper.

THE JUROR:

The housewife thinks she does not know much about young people,
not anymore. Girls together in combat boots running toward the
fire.

THE REPORTER:

And in the Public Mouth, such hues and cries, such drool and suck
at the facts, such hash and rehash. Did she engineer the kidnap?
Truly convert?

THE COMRADE (Yolanda):

Miserable runt that she was, she was
the fucking feather in the SLA's
thinking cap, a trophy, a goddamn smoked ham.
How were they going to show this piece?
So brilliant Cinque had himself a brainstorm:
since 1) Tania needed to be initiated, and 2)
they needed some bread and 3) the spotlight and 4) banks
exist as everyone fucking well knows to screw
the People, it was simple: rob one of them banks.

THE FAIRY GODMOTHER:

The princess was simply stunned by the possible.
She would sit in a trance at a tableful
of Elmer's glue and clocks and toaster wires
and think of deprivation's glamours.
She was looking for life, learning
to watch herself watch herself watching
shadows, curtains; learning
how to separate her heart forever
from its last beat, how to cover

everything unbearable with loud and louder
music. And then . . .

THE COMRADE (Yolanda):

She was weak as a steamed bean, our new comrade,
after screwing around in the closet so long.
She would have to appear as herself—too bad
they'd gone and chopped off that identifiable
hair, but she did have that shit-eating smile . . .
They studied their parts so nothing would go wrong.

THE FAIRY GODMOTHER:

The fairy godmother
pulled her shawl of wings around her.
At this point there was little
she could do but fiddle.

THE MOTHER:

Meanwhile, back at the palace, the king was morose
and methodical; he talked to his knights
of law and order, he talked to his knights
of the pen, now subject to their salable gush
as was the queen, who was sadly being proper
in her preoccupations. She worried about her

other daughters and kept them near.
She hardly spoke when the cameras whirred at her.

THE GIRLFRIEND:

Tania-in-waiting is busy dreaming
the rest of her life: sometimes in love sometimes pretending.
She dreams she enters her father's safe. It is heart-shaped,
and she knows the combination. She fills her sack with cash,
bills and coins stamped with her father's face
in whom she trusts and takes
pride until she wakes.

THE REPORTER:

Then one sporty morning in the land of Media Major the Gates of
Gazette blow wide and fill the Public Mouth. Presenting (con-
tinuous performances): *The Hibernia Bank Heist*, starring Tania
and the SLA dancers. The story is already taking its place beside that
Valentine's Day Jesse James showed how to tip a jug. And now as
then the Retinue of Report has a ball packaging the Event, passing
on the word of the bandit queen herself:

> *Greetings to the People: this is Tania. On April 15 my
> comrades and I expropriated $10,660.02 from the Sunset
> Branch of the Hibernia Bank. Casualties could have been
> avoided had the persons involved kept out of the way and
> co-operated with the People's forces until after the departure.*

THE COMRADE (Yolanda):

And thus one day in the year of the Soldier,
the People's Army, full of grace,

liberated certain supplies and cash (that was due
them from the filthy fascist pig capitalists who
had stolen it from the People in the first place).
And Tania was right there proving a little fascist cunt can grow up
to be a freedom fighter, even if she did screw up
when she forgot her speech. And if that civilian asshole
hadn't of seemed to be
                    fucking up the get-away
                              like one of them armed enemy
force elements they might of not
          had to shoot
                    but anyways, after all
the People was fucking amazed—
                    they knew, every damn one
that the Revolution had begun.

THE JUROR:

What does it feel like to be so special? The housewife had no idea.
Love is so foolish an evidence, guilt by astrology. What does it feel
like to walk right into a bank with a gun? A thrill too I'd say. But
what I really wonder is, were they glad to see each other again
after the robbery? Cujo and her? Did she do it out of love?

THE GIRLFRIEND:

She was sitting in the center of a circle
of soldiers with guns and grins on their faces
and they were stretching out their hands to her.
She was opening the sack of money like
a Christmas stocking. She was going to hand out
the booty like loaves and fishes. She shook
the sack upside down but no money fell out,

only pieces of broken glass, sharp spindles, a black
slilth as of snakes. As she scooped handfuls
blood ran down her arms to her elbows.
The People around her, hand to mouth like toddlers,
were stuffing themselves on dangerous hors d'oeuvres,
growing larger and larger like Alices
while she herself shrank and finally lay down
limp as a savaged inner tube, and she could feel
a comforting seep of sense from every cell . . .

THE MOTHER:

The land's chiefest knight of law and order
then called the princess a common criminal.
The king and queen did not believe their daughter
had had any choice in the matter at all.
They could see the guns of the Cobra People
pointed at her. They could hear the denial
behind her words, see her trapped in the middle.

THE GIRLFRIEND:

Waking at noon, Tania-in-waiting felt as if
    her life had changed forever.
    She couldn't look at her father
        as he looked up from his paper;

his cheeks were red, his eyes tough
and glinting sharply, cool as
broken glass.

THE REPORTER:

And the Public Mouth moves, tongues the same old opus from
cheek to cheek, grinds and grounds, sucks 'til the taste is ash. Quip-
less I quote the rant of Cinque Mtume:

> *And if white people in fascist America don't think they are
> enslaved, they only prove their own foolishness . . . Black
> people, more revolutionary than ever before, are armed and
> angry, and now the SLA is proving the Black People ain't
> alone, that the things the pigs have feared the most is happen-
> ing, is growing. A People's Army . . .*

THE COMRADE (Yolanda):

So Cinque was passing round the plum
wine and pink pancakes, celebrating the masses,
blessing the People: "the enemy knows who I am . . .
I am the bringer of the children of the oppressed
and the children of the oppressor together . . . I am
bringing the truth to the children . . ."
But there's a practical problem:
the fascist pig henchmen is all around

on the look-out for the front page faces
of the SLA; so they needs to keep their asses
to the ground.

THE GIRLFRIEND:

Tanias-in-waiting from princesses right down
to chambermaids, each safe in her bed,
each a secret just dying to be known,
a seed about to sprout, turn up and be loved.
She is wanted.

THE FAIRY GODMOTHER:

Fabula Grunt was beginning to feel
sick of her experiment, the buzz words *struggle,*
expropriation, consciousness,
liberation, venceremos . . .

THE COMRADE (Yolanda):

Their works has piled up in the teensy safehouse.
The closet where Tania raised her consciousness
was full of used-up words, plans, pamphlets,
clock parts and shit like that. So they gets
the bright idea to dump all this treasure
in the bathtub with two weeks of garbage, water,
ink, cyanide, and just a soupçon of piss from each
of them, a sort of personal touch.

THE FAIRY GODMOTHER:

And Fabula sees how the princess grins
as she learns how to pick over garbage cans
for fake ID's . . . She sees images: knives,
wigs and wastepapers of imperatives,
embarrassed zebras, a bowl of dead fish,
costumes, a guitar case crammed with bullets,
the one scummed People's toothbrush,
sugar in little packets . . .

THE COMRADE (Yolanda):

A fucking bonanza for the FBI.
And they leaves some writing on the wall:
in Tania's hand, PATRIA O MUERTE . . .
Then Gelina the actress fix them all
up in greasy blackface, all except Cin
of course, and they begins to fight over
who gets to look at theirselves in
the bathroom mirror.

THE FAIRY GODMOTHER:

All a fairy godmother could do at this point
was to watch them with a sinking heart,
watch the princess hug her carbine, hum Mozart,
rather pleased with the nursery smell of greasepaint,
the burnt almond of cyanide . . .

THE REPORTER:

A little legwork in order, I mooch down with my tinstar friend to
that forgone funk hole on Golden Gate. There it is: *"Death to the
fascist insect that preys on the life of the People." "Venceremos!"*
Blah blah. But talk about pigs! I wouldn't take a second noseful of
that wallow if I didn't smell the story in it.

THE FAIRY GODMOTHER:

Fabula was beside herself here;
she was seeing ahead now, it was all too clear:
she was going to have to interfere . . .

THE COMRADE (Yolanda):

Hunkered down now in a new safehouse
    in a downstage good-rap type
        neighborhood of the People
the SLA began training for real
        for the coming struggle.
Cinque divided them up
    into three combat units of three each
        so they could perfect their search-
and-destroy strategies.
    Tania was getting so she could handle
        her gun and move her ass.

THE FAIRY GODMOTHER:

Between the warp of sight and weft of wisdom
the new cloth of revision grew:
she had to get the princess away from them.

THE COMRADE (Yolanda):

One day Cinque ordered the combat unit
of Yolanda and Teko and Tania
    to take some of the fucking Hibernia
    expropriation to buy some shit
  they needed from this sports type
                store way away
from their safehouse.
           They was to if busted re-group
at the drive-in just in case . . .

THE REPORTER:

I've played my share of Hide and Seek, know some mice way down
the line, but they're all huggermugger (lovely word) as far as this
SLA caper goes. I'm getting sick of red herring here and there a
crank call, myopic witnesses . . .

THE FAIRY GODMOTHER:

Timing, that was the main thing.
When the fairy godmother saw
that Teko and Yolanda were leaving
the princess in the van her thought
moved with the possibilities . . .
    While Teko was still browsing
    in the aisles and Yolanda paying
    cash, Fabula caught Teko looking
    at a bandolier. "Why pay?" she thought for him,
    "stick it up your sleeve in the name
    of the People." He did. Fabula then turned
    the eye of a clerk toward Teko
    at that moment, and as the comrades were

walking out, Teko felt a hand
clap his shoulder . . .

THE COMRADE (Yolanda):

Shit! It went utterly
    fucking wrong. How were they
        supposed to know that pig-rigged store
            was full of enemy assholes? Gunfire
        was the only thing could free
            them from a fucking torture chamber
in the fascist prisons of Amerikkka.
Surprised the piss
            out of Teko and Yolanda
how Tania fucking saved the day—
    she pulled the trigger,
the little cunt come across.

THE FAIRY GODMOTHER:

So the fairy godmother's first plan—
arrest—fell through. When she saw it was
inevitable, she did her best to assist
the mad dash. Now to abandon the van . . .

THE REPORTER:

Just when I'm about to hallucinate for lack of a lead, bingo! This
call comes through the static, sets my story going again like a house
afire. The star of my opus is outside this sporting goods store shooting the hell out of the curb with a submachine gun . . .

THE MOTHER:

She was shooting and racing off
with the Cobra People, glad she was alive
horrified . . .

THE REPORTER:

Wanted by the FBI, nearly caught shoplifting—who could make
this up?

THE GIRLFRIEND:

Neither Tania nor Tania-in-waiting was meant for this.

THE JUROR:

Apart from Cujo. I sure do not know how to think about that one.
It doesn't fit in.

THE COMRADE (Yolanda):

And then by a perilous route
    that took a whole fucking night
        waiting at the drive-in with a brand
new expropriated car, the van abandoned,
the three comrades arrived at Disneyland.
    They couldn't wait to just hang out
        with the asshole tourists all gaga at that
bourgeois Mickey Mouse pigshit.

THE REPORTER:

So I am right there when they peg the dumped van with right there in the front seat a parking ticket with an address. Before you can say royal flush, everyone flocks to this street in the slums. The first shack they surround is empty, but the neighbors tell where this crazy mother and his white girlfriends are flattened out—bonanza! and a big question mark: is Tania inside? Patty? The dicks are calling and calling through their big bullhorns to come out, come out . . .

THE COMRADE (Yolanda):

There they was in this incredible
bourgeois room—matching bedspreads and curtains,
a sanitary paper seal
on the crapper, a fucking color T.V., visions
of conspicuous consumption.
Amused, they flick on
the set, and there's this incredible
scene, this little house . . .

THE MOTHER:

The king's men called out again and again.
Shadows maundered at windows, bickered in curtains
front and back; and back and forth the guns
talked death to death. Popcorn, she thought,
it sounded like the hot crescendos
of popcorn . . .

THE COMRADE (Yolanda):

The three cooped up in that fucking motel
knew their comrades would never come out.
They was the habitués of hell.
Barely breathing, they watched and thought
they saw the dark silhouette
of their beloved General Field Marshal
behind a curtain. Tania thought
Cujo's gun was visible
for a second . . .
                    The enemy tossed
bombs from all sides until . . .

THE GIRLFRIEND:

Tania-in-waiting was glued to the set like a clairvoyant
to a crystal ball, witnessing the death that was meant
for her. At first there were just slight puffs of smoke,
a dragon breathing normally, then hot spurts, like
a dragon sneezing, and then the dragon, like a doomed
dirigible . . . She shut her eyes and almost screamed.

THE COMRADE (Yolanda):

. . . the house was a fireball. In living color
the People's forces watched that shitload
of Amerikkkan violence come down on the heads

of their loved ones, and they seen for sure
that Cinque Mtume's prophecies were true.

THE REPORTER:

I stay on the scene, gutsick and dumbfounded while the king's men
sift the ashes, scrutinize bits of the blackened remains. Black at last,
fused to their bandoliers, busted by their own flack. Then this one
dick holds up a little something from the wreck, a little trophy. Still
ticking. I am thinking, the deadline. And will Tania's or Patty's
smile be found among the teeth?

THE GIRLFRIEND:

Remains. Tania-in-waiting
    remains as the old names are given
        to the plastic sacks of tooth and bone,
            names going back to the christening
                of each, names to be buried in . . .
But Tania remains, Tania-in-waiting
remains, alive and buried in the living
    beyond herself, a kind
        of Phoenix . . .

THE MOTHER:

The queen grew more shivery,
wore her grief like unmentionable surgery.
Qualms and questions, the touch-and-go grief
did not purify like finalities.
The king sent sadness out of his eyes.

224

THE COMRADE (Yolanda):

Yolanda wrote to the People:

"*It's hard to explain what it was like watching our comrades die . . . a battalion of pigs facing a fire team of guerrillas, and the only way they could defeat them was to burn them alive . . . Cinque loved the people with tenderness and respect . . . it's not how long we live, he used to say, it's how we live.*"

THE FAIRY GODMOTHER:

After the fire, the fairy godmother gave Tania
a new name: Pearl. Teko thought it was he
who thought of it. He and Yolanda became Frank and Eva,
and Fabula arranged for the three to be
driven to a secret place far away.

THE GIRLFRIEND:

At first I could look no one in the eyes
for fear they would recognize
Tania, for fear the world would burst
into flame . . .

THE JUROR:

I kept thinking of that sentence from the SLA eulogy tape: "*We mourn together and the sounds of gunfire grow sweeter.*" I don't get it, but it's beautiful to say, like in a book.

THE FAIRY GODMOTHER:

Fabula left Teko and Yolanda to their perfidious
delusions, but she placed a sharp seed of doubt
like a sliver of glass in the heart of the Princess
around which secret the new sense of Pearl could accrete.
A truer identity Fabula kept safe in her pocket,
a thin spindle starving for new twists of wool
to be spun to a fine long yarn to fatten it.
And Fabula made the princess able
to understand she was no longer Tania pretending
to be Pearl, but Pearl pretending to be Tania,
and the power to play and to keep on playing
lay in the charm, the abracadabra
Fabula invested in the little Olmec monkey
Cujo gave the princess when she took the name
of Tania. Now all that was left of the revolutionary
spell, with the death of the evil Cinque Mtume,
was a time in hiding, a melting away,
a gradual remembering—it could take a year and a day.

THE COMRADE (Yolanda):

Way the hell out in the pretty boondocks
where only sick-assed capitalists can afford to go
for R & R, the brave remnant of the Malcolm X
Combat Unit of the SLA lay low.
They ran in circles to keep in shape
and got on each other's nerves like any family cooped up.
They chewed half-sticks of gum to practice poverty,
began to write a history
of the deeds of the SLA and Cinque.

THE REPORTER:

Hide and seek. A missing person story—hot by dint of a feel for the fictional. I nibble brass tacks, skulldrag it, reckon it and s'pose. I go shopping. Nothing. I am sick of the five W's and their shrugs. A cipher, she leaves me speechless. Even from her childhood she was missing. Why should I mother this nothing?

THE MOTHER:

Every day the queen said to herself,
  this day will pass, and it did,
but not the long season of winter
  in which she wondered and waited.
The wait made her think of a mustard seed
  in a crystal dollop, defied
to sprout. It was beyond words, like
  the sadness of a child who can't yet speak.
No birthdays were celebrated, no
  anniversaries, no holidays, no
mirrors flattered. Charities
  languished, memories tarnished, no
locks responded to their keys.

THE JUROR:

And after all she had no place to go, that's the way I understood it at the trial. No wonder she had the bull-horrors, and no wonder she kept the little stone monkey. Her lover was burned up, she was with those other two, just them. They were not the most sensitive people. The Missing Year. There were hints something was rotten

in the Missing Year. Otherwise why the Fifth Amendment? If I
was her I wouldn't remember either.

THE FAIRY GODMOTHER:

The secret place was full of sun
and blueberries, and in the wrought iron
gate was P-A-I-X. Ponds, windmills, sudden
thunderstorms. And Fabula brought one
of her other fugitive godchildren—
her name was Wendy and she would become
an important part of Fabula's plan.

THE GIRLFRIEND:

I dreamed my father leaned over
the glass coffin in which I lay.
His eyes were dimes; he squinted as if to see . . .
. . . and then I was dreaming of Beauty
    taken by the Beast in exchange
    for the sins of her father, a sacrifice,
    yet she found herself wanting to please . . .
    She was wanted. Everything changed.
    She listened to the Beast
    and while he whispered to her he changed
    into a little stone monkey
    she could hold in her hand.

THE FAIRY GODMOTHER:

In bright light Pearl played Tania still
    and moved her body to Teko's drill
        and moved her lips around a script,

while in dark and cover of thunder she felt
secret and safe in a soft gathering of wool.

THE GIRLFRIEND:

I woke up and thought
about my two dreams all day.
The next night I dreamed I found a note
from Tania in our old secret
place where we used to play.
It said: we are women and women
must not throw themselves before swine.

THE FAIRY GODMOTHER:

Fabula put it into their heads finally
to return to the birthplace of the SLA
and saw to it that Pearl and Wendy
lived together apart from the hideaway
of the others . . .
And Wendy and Pearl talked of being sisters
closer than crossed fingers.
Pearl still had the monkey in her purse,
but she was coming very close
to not needing it, the spell unraveling . . .
and Tania? Tania was not at home
where Pearl and Wendy were living.
It was almost time.

THE GIRLFRIEND:

She daydreamed in the kitchen:
herself beside her old playmate

who was writing a letter to her lover
and she did not even have to ask what
was in it, she knew naturally . . .
and suddenly two thugs were at the door
with guns shouting "FREEZE. FBI.
FREEZE!"
                    It jolted her
back to herself, the empty kitchen,
and she began to weep for the friend
that was not there.

THE JUROR:

What I thought about more than anything else at the trial was how
she wet her pants when those officers broke into her apartment
shouting to freeze. It can happen to anyone: it is a very desperate
giveaway to how you feel when no power is left in you.

THE MOTHER:

When at long last she was caught,
the unhappy princess was taken straight
to jail and chained as the law of the land
required, even for the spellbound
daughters of kings. The queen, stunned,
put on a black dress to visit the jail, and then
remembered to put some color on.

THE REPORTER:

My electrified tripewriter is chuckling at me once more as I puzzle
the apparition of her raised fist. The end in sight, I am no longer out
of town in a trance. The body's in the box, the story is in it, but
there's still a missing person at the center. I will be sentencing again.

THE COMRADE (Yolanda):

Me and Tania was in the fucking jail
    together, but our eyes didn't meet exactly.
Did that shitface tip off the pigs? Was just me
    and Teko going to be tortured,
        pins under our fingernails? I heard
    her give her occupation as "urban
        guerrilla," but that sly-ass smile
she gave with it wasn't nothing to believe in.

THE MOTHER:

The queen arrived at the jail with an armload
of yellow roses and white orchids, as if flowers
might break the evil spell. She brought tears
and the promise of forgetfulness, the real world
of silk and Shalimar in her embrace; she wanted
to brush away the enchantment forever
like mist from a mirror.

Scuttlebutt, grapevine, muck, all tongue work: fury and glee. And
F. Lee Bailey is said to be the starlight, mender of the defenses.
What a court-crash it's going to be, what copy! I am about to lose
myself in a litter of prediction. But what I want right now more
than mother love is a sweet tête-à-tête with the lamb. Nix, natch.
She is circum-surrounded already with stopless mouthpieces, shrink-
age experts, linguists numbering the loves and fuck-yous she has
uttered.

THE MOTHER:

The queen couldn't see why, after all
the horrors of hell with the Cobra People,
her daughter should stand trial.
The king could, despite his pain.
After all, he said, this is a land
of law and order and equality.
The royal family would stand
trial as well as any.

THE GIRLFRIEND:

Yes, they let me in,
nothing but everything between
us. I couldn't be sure . . . I mean,
        she looked so starved, ghostly
                even, and that red hair . . .
Like her eyes didn't see me
        talking that breathless street-patter.
We should have guessed the feds
        were taping it. The words

came out gray, like used dishwater,
    underpants not in their prime.
I went home
    and took a bath in my own name.

THE COMRADE (Yolanda):

So here's Tania and me in cells side by side,
but Tania is turning back into the simple
wimp of a pigfaced princess she had been
before her liberation.
                        Motherfucking ungrateful,
singing all the shit she can
think of, fingering . . .
                        I can feel
the walls of my heart drip with acid.
Back there on the farm why the hell
didn't Teko and me just go ahead
and waste that bitch whiles we could?

THE MOTHER:

There came to be a comforting litany
on the queen's tongue: Judgment, Exoneration, Purification:
words smooth and comforting as the Spanish sherry
in the cellars of San Simeon.

THE REPORTER:

Welcome to "The Patty Hearst Show." As the great front man himself has been heard to say: "Look, a trial is a play. It's not a matter

of who is right and who is wrong. It's giving the jurors a play they can relate to."

THE JUROR:

So in jail obviously she has told this story over and over to the mind-doctors—I get this feeling—but she doesn't tell them about her love. No, she doesn't tell, they have to steal the little monkey out of her purse. They dangle it in front of her there in the court-room. It had to be that she loved him to keep it so long.

THE MOTHER:

The queen is in the front row
in the courtroom. She smiles
a far-off smile, a winter smile
beginning to thaw . . .

THE REPORTER:

Between the hustle and hype, the tears and vomit, what they all want is a story. There she is, pale as Wonder Bread, boxed in but inventing herself still, urging us to make sense and consequence out of the word-wreckage. In the closet, in the garbage can, the jail cell, the witness box, the frame of the nightly news, of *Time* . . . Locked in and no Houdini; nor am I, to get out of my own trap . . .

THE MOTHER:

This is a rude season for us.
I watch myself watch myself

watching over. I cover her
in linen, silk, velvet. How thin
she is, slip of philodendron,
eyes bigger than they used to be,
not eyes but bruises . . .

THE GIRLFRIEND:

I testify as to who I am
    and that she is as close to me
        as I am, closer.
She helped hold up my father's bank,
    and I would do the same, I think,
        to save my life.
                    She made me
see what matters. Once more
close, we do not lie.
    Either we are not guilty
        or both of us are.

THE JUROR:

She looks quite pitiful, but she looks guilty, too. I will be glad when
all this thinking is over. I will even be glad to see my husband late
at night. But when the twelve of us have got all of the story we are
going to get and we are sent out together, I am thinking that this
feeling will never be over, this feeling that it happened to me.

THE REPORTER:

She is chained to right and left to be the flimsiest evidence to the
fact that she is . . . the fiction that she is, in fact, made up. Tugged

between the fathoms of babble and the scribblements of the press, between squabbles and boredom (while the judge catches some shut-eye), she is nothing and everything I can imagine: princess cutie dolorosa doll star bitch bandit victim femme futile Miss Etcetera Industries . . . what you make of her. Heroine or judasgoat, transumed in the crucible of hoopla, trinket terrorist, my bread and butter, oh, I could go on with her . . .

THE MOTHER:

I sit at the spectacle
of my daughter, this cat's cradle
of expert threads and theory
I cannot untangle
for the life of me.

THE FAIRY GODMOTHER:

Now the fairy godmother was
utterly flustrated at the trial.
She could hardly tell hit from miss,
fussed up as she was, a cook surrounded
with sudden mouths, her cupboard full
of contrary ingredients. The fetid
air was thick—a minestrone of opinion, a stew
of scraps and buffalo—

steam blown all around.
Some lids she clapped on,
                          some she took off.
    Roast here, grill
    there. Here some beef
            there a clam; a bluff
of something, a dash of lemon . . .
                          she was busier than
    a witch at midnight.

THE COMRADE (Yolanda) :

So I am rotting in this decrepit
    funk-box, fucking upstrung in the daily blab—
        the noosepaper, I call it—
while Marie Antoinette is hot shit.
        She gets to hob-nob
with pigs in suits. Who thinks about
    the hungry children, the political scapegoat
like me, the passion that we lived? Where does
    it end? I've got the blood
    of Emily on my hands, cornfed
chickenshit cheerleader that she was.
        How many need to be killed
before . . . ? That bitch! That pig bitch killed
    Tania. Fuck you, Tania, my own
mistake of creation.

THE JUROR:

Finally, finally they are coming to an end. The judge wakes up and instructs us. We crowd into the windowless room, the twelve of us. Somebody called us prisoners of justice. We do not look left or right. I understand love, but still it would have been wrong of me in the eyes of God to defy the law of my country for love. Wouldn't it? I don't know . . .

THE MOTHER:

Too many secrets behind her
smile. But it is too late
now to unteach that bo-peep,
that kind of perdu, quick sleight
of lip we learn on Mother's lap
from Mother's milk. They find her
guilty
and of that smile she is
and so am I.

THE REPORTER:

It is over, post-partum, post mortem. I have found the missing person. She is locked into the alphabet like a tongue. It comes to me: the alphabet is a kind of murder mystery. I am undone by what I put into my mouth. The body of evidence is there in bloody black and white: story complete with angles and curves, fat padding the moving muscles, marrow in the picked syntactical bones.

THE JUROR:

I hear that because of me she is going to jail for seven years, and
I try not to think about it. I bury myself in stories that turn out the
way they are supposed to.

THE GIRLFRIEND:

She is going to be pardoned for her nightmares.
She is going to start all over being herself
as I am.

THE MOTHER:

The princess, stripped of name after
    name, shipped from prison to prison, no more
        than a number and no less than a number
of daughters. I pray:
May I, may she, may the stranger
be safe from the daughterless winter.

THE GIRLFRIEND:

She will marry her bodyguard, and I
will marry mine. As our hands are given
we uncross our fingers, uncross our hearts.
We do not hope to die.

THE COMRADE (Yolanda):

We need to fucking live in death, sister
bitch, and so happily never-never after

THE COMRADE (Emily):

that day I gave up childhood for the love
of pirates, the love of the lost, remember?

THE JUROR:

And I read in *The Star* how she was pardoned by the President
himself. She is back with the brave and free and my burden lifts.
And her lucky prince, imagine, raised from nowhere to a fortune.
After the bad dream comes the everyday: casseroles and laundry
and the kissable avocado pit sprouted in the dark closet. She will
know how I feel.

THE FAIRY GODMOTHER:

The fairy godmother took her place
among the anonymous Mother Tongues,
the inscrutables whose rights were sometimes wrongs
and vice versa. Though it lacked a certain grace,
her story was praised for its equivocal
spur to the confab. It was said it might be
a late gestation or a cipher;
    it might be a chimney
sweeping after a chimney fire;

it might be a rending of all
   or an entangling or a key;
it must be a devil's tale,
   as all original tales must be.

THE REPORTER:

I am a mouth beneath all. Bring me a small bowl of everything from the crazy salad bar! O, glutteral knowledge, O, black white and red, we are born only to stutter out in the end like a candle in the wind. Forgive me, Mother.

THE FAIRY GODMOTHER:

The riddle is red.
Her story is mine.
It is time for bed.

About the Author

Pamela White Hadas was born in Holland, Michigan, in 1946.
She is the author of three books of poems, *The Passion of
Lilith, Designing Women,* and *In Light of Genesis,* and of a
study of Marianne Moore. She has taught at Washington
University in St. Louis, Missouri, Middlebury College, and the
Bread Loaf Writers' Conference. She and her husband, David
Hadas, live in St. Louis.

A Note on the Type

The text of this book was set in Intertype Garamond No. 3, a
modern rendering of the type first cut by Claude Garamond
(1510–1561). Garamond was a pupil of Geoffroy Troy and is
believed to have based his letters on the Venetian models,
although he introduced a number of important differences, and
it is to him we owe the letter which we know as old-style. He
gave to his letters a certain elegance and a feeling of movement
that won for their creator an immediate reputation and the
patronage of Francis I of France.

Composed by Maryland Linotype Composition Company,
Baltimore, Maryland
Printed and bound by Kingsport Press, Kingsport, Tennessee
Typography and binding design by Virginia Tan